Key issues for secondary schools

WITHDRAWN

Key Issues for Secondary Schools addresses the main issues in secondary education and their implications for schools. It is presented in a convenient A to Z format, which enables readers to quickly find topics of immediate or particular interest.

Includes essential information on:

- accreditation of pupils
- careers education and guidance
- discipline
- leadership and management
- transition from primary to secondary school.

ch section ends with a series of points for action, selective suggestions r further reading and addresses of useful contacts. It is intended for a de range of people professionally concerned with education, from head- achers and governors to BEd and PGCE students. It is a reference book at no secondary school should be without.

Michael Farrell trained as a teacher and research psychologist and has worked as a headteacher and a lecturer at the University of London, nstitute of Education. He has directed national education projects and s the author of *Key Issues for Primary Schools*, also published by outledgeFalmer.

Key issues for primary schools

Michael Farrell

'This book makes a valuable contribution to analysing, clarifying, coding and assisting . . . primary professionalism.'
    – Professor Colin Richards, former HMI for Primary Education, University College of St Martin

Key Issues for Primary Schools is a concise comprehensive guide to the main issues in primary education and the implications for schools. Presented in a convenient A–Z format, the book includes coverage of:

- special educational needs
- attendance, truancy and exclusion
- bullying and behavioural problems
- management and administration
- safety and security.

There is also a review of up-to-date DfEE requirements and suggestions for further action and reading. The addresses of useful contacts help to make it a reference book no primary school should be without.

1999: 234x156: 224pp
Pb: 0–415–18262–X: £16.99

Key issues for secondary schools

Michael Farrell

Foreword by Professor Trevor Kerry

London and New York

First published 2001
by RoutledgeFalmer
11 New Fetter Lane, London EC4P 4EE

Simultaneously published in the USA and Canada
by RoutledgeFalmer
29 West 35th Street, New York, NY 10001

RoutledgeFalmer is an imprint of the Taylor & Francis Group

© 2001 Michael Farrell

Typeset in Sabon by
Florence Production Ltd, Stoodleigh, Devon
Printed and bound in Great Britain by
TJ International Ltd, Padstow, Cornwall.

British Library Cataloguing in Publication Data
A catalogue record for this book is available from the British Library

Library of Congress Cataloging in Publication Data
Farrell, Michael, 1948–
Key issues for secondary schools / Michael Farrell; foreword by
Trevor Kerry.
p. cm.
Includes bibliographical references (p.)
ISBN 0–415–23255–4 (pbk. : alk. paper)
1. Education, Secondary—Great Britain.   I. Title.
LA635.F37 2001
373.41–dc21   00–045734

ISBN 0–415–23255–4

This book is dedicated to my dear daughter Anne, aged 16, my secondary school consultant.

Contents

Foreword

We live in an increasingly knowledge-dominated society, yet one in which the most precious commodity of all – time – seems to become ever more elusive. Nowhere are these phenomena more evident than in the world of education. Professionals are under enormous pressure from the government to achieve more and more with a diminishing resource. At the same time many, like school governors, give freely of their time and expertise to support a system that places on them increasing burdens without any hint of reward.

This book seeks to alleviate some of the problems of time by providing knowledge about secondary education and the school system in a compact, concise, yet authoritative format so that busy professionals can access that knowledge without spending more time than is necessary trawling the internet or searching through libraries.

Michael Farrell has a long and very varied experience as an educator and as an author. This volume is typical of his work in that it is designed to sift, from a plethora of data, the key ideas and then to present them in a sound and straightforward way. The result is not only a mine of information, but also a readable and accessible volume.

Key Issues for Secondary Schools will give the reader a rapid, yet incisive grasp of those major topics that form the agenda of secondary education in the early years of the twenty-first century.

Professor Trevor Kerry
Vice President of the College of Teachers
Lincoln
May 2000

Acknowledgements

I am most grateful to the following people who read sections of the book and made many helpful suggestions.

From the Department for Education and Employment

Mr Trevor Anguin, Pupil Support and Independent Schools Division; Ms Dawn Faniku, Pupil Performance and Research Team; Ms Janice Lawson, School Improvement Division; Mr Ian Thompson, School Attendance and Disadvantaged Pupils Team; Mr Ashley Howarth-Robert, Discipline and Exclusions Team.

From other organisations

Mr David Andrews, Careers Education and Guidance Consultant and Trainer, Hertfordshire Careers Services Ltd.; Ms Antoinette Agbodohu, Child Protection Assistant Policy Co-ordinator, Department of Health; Mr Peter Carey, Director, National Association for Gifted Children; Mr Nick Chambers, Institute of Development Professionals in Education; Mr Peter Rudd, Senior Research Officer, School Improvement Research Centre, National Foundation for Educational Research; Dr Marianne Talbot, Brasenose College, Oxford; Mr Tim Toulmin, Press Complaints Commission; Mr Peter Jackson, Qualifications and Curriculum Authority.

Professor Trevor Kerry, Vice President of the College of Teachers, and Mr Rob Gwynne, Principal, Long Sands College, Cambridgeshire, read the whole manuscript and made many helpful comments.

I am grateful to all the colleagues who read and commented on earlier drafts of the text. Their assistance does not indicate that the people or organisations involved endorse or necessarily agree with anything in the text. Nor does the inclusion of an address at the end of a section indicate that members of that organisation agree with or endorse anything in the preceding section. The address is a source of further information and does not indicate that any documents listed in references or further reading can be obtained from the address.

Where references are given to a publication prepared by an organisation, the name of the organisation as it was at the time of the publication is given. For example, the present Department for Education and Employment has had several previous titles so a publication made when the Department was, say, the Department of Education is cited with that earlier Department name.

The information and views expressed in *Key Issues for Secondary Schools* are my personal views and do not represent the views of any organisation. Any shortcomings of the book are, of course, entirely my own.

Introduction

Readers of this book

I was most encouraged that my earlier book, *Key Issues for Primary Schools*, published by Routledge in 1999, was generously reviewed by the media and well received by readers. The present volume is a companion book for the secondary phase. It is intended for a wide range of people professionally concerned with education: aspirant school leaders, head-teachers, teachers, governors, Office for Standards in Education inspectors, local education authority inspectors, advisers, officers and support staff. Equally, it is intended for educators in universities and colleges of higher education, students in training doing Bachelor of Education (BEd) or Post-Graduate Certificate in Education (PGCE) courses. Finally, the book will be useful to teachers on professional development courses (including management courses) and postgraduate Master of Education (MEd) courses, and civil servants involved in education.

Format of the book

The book comprises entries on key issues presented in alphabetical order. The title of each section has been chosen so that the first word of the title gives a clear indication of the content of the section. Consequently, the alphabetical listing of sections also acts as an index, enabling readers to find quickly topics of immediate or particular interest.

Uses of the book

Key Issues for Secondary Schools gives a series of briefings on a wide range of topics. Because the book is aimed predominantly at professionals, a certain level of readership knowledge is assumed that enables it to cover issues in some depth in a relatively short space. The book sets out to offer practical help while stimulating debate on the issues concerned. Many of the entries will inform staff in schools as they prepare and develop policies, guidelines and practice.

Key points in the text are identified by bullet marks and lists. Towards the end of each entry is a list of suggestions about what the school should be doing. A small number of references is given (and occasionally further reading). Addresses and telephone numbers, fax numbers and e-mail addresses are given as appropriate for further information or for useful contacts.

Addresses

Addresses are given at the end of each section. To avoid undue repetition, however, addresses from which publications can be ordered are given below:

> Department for Education and Employment Publications, PO Box 5050, Sherwood Park, Annesley, Nottinghamshire NG15 0DJ, tel: 0845 6022 260, fax: 01623 759 045, e-mail: dfee@prologistics.co.uk
>
> Office for Standards in Education Publications Centre, PO Box 6927, London E3 3NZ, tel: 020 7510 0180.
>
> The Stationery Office, 51 Nine Elms Lane, London SW8 5DR, tel: 020 7873 8280.

Suggestions

I would be pleased to hear from readers with suggestions for amendments or additions so that future editions of the book will continue to be as informative as possible. Please write to me, Dr Michael Farrell, care of the publishers or by e-mail: michael@educatio.demon.uk

Accreditation of pupil achievement

Balancing relevance and cohesiveness

Charles Caleb Colton, the British clergyman, regarded examinations as, 'formidable, even to the best prepared, for the greatest fool may ask more than the wisest man can answer'. As well as this timely reminder of what every student facing assessment knows, there is the added issue of conveying to students the nature of the national system of accreditation and qualifications, which is still something of a labyrinth even to educators.

Some have argued persuasively for a more transparent and open-ended system. For example, Bloomer (1997), drawing on various sources including the Leverhulme Study, criticises the search for uniformity of outcome and top-down approaches. Instead, he argues for an approach that emphasises such things as professionalism and diversity in educational practice. However, for employers, students, teachers and others a cohesive and comprehensible system has advantages. At the very least, unless students can grasp the system, it is difficult for them to see the options open to them and the different routes of progression which are possible.

An important issue is the development of a framework in which vocational and 'academic' qualifications can be described, understood, contrasted, compared and fitted together. Attempts have been made to broadly compare the levels of achievement represented by General National Vocational Qualifications (GNVQs) and National Vocational Qualifications (NVQs) with those represented by qualifications in General Certificate of Secondary Education (GCSE) and Advanced level (A level) and Advanced Supplementary level (AS level) qualifications. These help employers and others compare the levels of different qualifications and allow students to use one set of qualifications to lead to courses involving other qualifications. The Qualifications and Curriculum Authority (QCA), however, recognise that comparisons should be made bearing in mind the different stuctures and purposes of the qualifications in the framework. For instance, while NVQs are a work-based qualification recognising what a person can do, school- or college-based GNVQs develop skills and knowledge in a vocational area.

Entry level, the first stratum of the national framework for qualifications, covers a range of subjects. These include art, business studies, child care, design and technology, food studies, English, French, geography and German. Also covered are hairdressing, history, information technology, land studies, leisure and tourism, mathematics, motor vehicle and road user studies, music, physical education, retail, and science. Entry level awards, for pupils who are not yet ready for GCSE, Foundation GNVQs or NVQ level 1 in a particular subject or area of study, are nationally recognised qualifications. They are accredited by the QCA and its partner bodies in Wales and Northern Ireland.

Three levels of Entry Level awards can be achieved, generally in line with national curriculum levels 1 to 3. Most entry level awards can be taken by pupils aged fourteen or older although for health and safety or legal reasons some courses may only be taken by pupils aged sixteen and over. Entry level awards can be taken at school alongside GCSE or GNVQ units or, at school or college, the awards may be taken alongside NVQ or GNVQ. A Certificate of Achievement offers National Curriculum accreditation at levels 1, 2 and 3 after a two-year course.

The common routes of progression in school are still:

- GCSE (two-year courses beginning in Year 10 of compulsory schooling) leading to A and AS levels (normally lasting two years in a wide range of mainly academic subjects and beginning in Year 12 of post compulsory education); and
- GNVQ Foundation, Intermediate and Advanced courses (broadly based vocational qualifications in areas such as leisure and tourism, art and design, and business).

Foundation GNVQ (usually a one-year course) is considered the equivalent of GCSE grades D–G; Intermediate GNVQ (normally a one-year course) is equivalent to GCSE grades A*–C; and Advanced GNVQ (usually a two-year course) is equivalent to two A-level passes. Accordingly, the usual school routes of progression are being increasingly enriched through possible progression from GCSE grades D–G to Intermediate GNVQ, from GCSE grades A–C to Advanced GNVQ and from GCSE to the International Baccalaureate. The International Baccalaureate, offered in a number of colleges and school sixth forms, is taken in place of A levels or Advanced GNVQ for entry into higher education. More widely based than are A levels, in the International Baccalaureate six subjects must be taken with three or four at advanced level and the rest at subsidiary level. Additionally, students write an extended essay, complete a course on the theory of knowledge, and carry out extracurricular activities. Also, GCSE short courses cover half the curriculum of a full GCSE and are 'worth' half a GCSE. Part one GNVQs, increasingly used to offer a vocational option alongside GCSEs in Years 10 and 11, can be taken at foundation or intermediate level and like full GNVQs cover a range of vocational areas.

At college, the usual progression is from:

- GCSE to A and AS levels;
- GNVQ Foundation to GNVQ Intermediate and GNVQ Advanced; and
- NVQ1 to NVQ2 and NVQ3.

Further flexibility is offered through other possible routes. These include progression from:

- GNVQ Foundation to NVQ2;
- GCSE grades D–G to GNVQ Intermediate and then to NVQ3; and
- GCSE grades A–C to GNVQ Advanced.

Also, the International Baccalaureate may take the place of A levels or Advanced GNVQ. The International Baccalaureate, A and AS levels and GNVQ Advanced can lead to entry into University or College where Higher National Diploma or first degree courses are taken.

In work, the usual progression route is through NVQ levels 1–5. Level 1, the foundation level, is equivalent to GCSE grades D–G. The NVQ level 2, craft level, is equivalent to four GCSEs grade A*–C. The NVQ level 3, technical level, is equivalent to two A levels or to GNVQ Advanced. All NVQs are job-specific courses, usually practically biased and involving demonstrating competence in certain areas.

National Traineeships is a work-based national scheme leading to an NVQ level 3 qualification. Modern Apprenticeships, intended for 16–24-year-olds, involve a programme usually lasting three years, which may include day release to college. Modern Apprenticeships lead to an NVQ level 3 qualification and are offered in a range of occupations such as social work or computer engineering.

Different awards draw on key skills (communication, application of number, information technology, working with others, improving own learning and performance, and problem solving). In GNVQ, the key skills of communication, application of number and information technology are compulsory. Key skills are part of Modern Apprenticeships and National Traineeships and are an optional part of the New Deal. The key skills of communication, application of number and information technology became available as a stand-alone qualification for A level, NVQ and GNVQ candidates from the year 2000.

At a national level, some simplification took place in 1998 when former examination boards combined into three Unitary Awarding Bodies (UAB) which award A levels, GCSEs and GNVQs. The University of London Examinations and Assessment Council (ULEAC) and the Business and

Technician Education Council (BTEC) became EdExel. The Oxford and Cambridge Board and the Royal Society of Arts (RSA) became OCR. The Associated Examining Board (AEB), the City and Guilds of London Institute (CGLI) and the Northern Examinations and Assessment Board (NEAB) became the Assessment and Qualifications Alliance (AQA). A national key-skills specification developed by the Qualifications and Curriculum Authority is delivered by the UABs and applies to GCSEs, A levels, GNVQs and NVQs.

GCSEs have a single- or two-tier system of entry to try to ensure that the level of work is pitched according to the appropriate level of prior learning. The exception is mathematics GCSE which has a three-tier system of entry. From September 2000, A level students started with three to five AS level courses, each comprising three AS modules which may be examined in the first year. Students then continue some subjects by taking three further 'A2' modules which lead to A level awards. From 2002, the brightest students may take 'world class' tests for 9-year-olds, 11-year-olds and for A level students where the tests are called the Advanced Extension examination.

Another force for cohesion and comprehensibility at the individual level is the National Record of Achievement. This tool for people to plan their learning and development is a folder in which learners keep their own histories of education, training and employment, their achievements and qualifications and their future development plans. The record contains details of the individual students' achievements, which may be academic, vocational, or personal.

Accreditation may take the form of qualifications and awards following examinations or continuing assessment or it may involve an ongoing record of pupil achievements. The more formal and nationally based the structure, the more likely it is that the accreditation will be understood and valued by employers and others. The more flexible and variable the accreditation, the more likely it is that others will be confused but the more flexible approaches may be more appealing to less able and less motivated students. Consequently, a difficult balance has to be struck between meeting the educational needs of students but not creating a system that is so complex and variable as to be largely incomprehensible.

The school is advised to consider:

- the various routes of progression and the relative value of different levels of qualification;
- maintaining a balance in the school between flexibility and cohesiveness in courses;
- ensuring that students are clear about the range of courses, their perceived value to employers and others, and the various routes of progression; and

- using National Records of Achievement as a means of helping students draw together their achievements.

References

Bloomer, M. (1997) *Curriculum Making in Post-16 Education: The social conditions of studentship*, London, Routledge.

Further reading

Farrell, M., Kerry, T. and Kerry, C. (1995) *The Blackwell Handbook of Education*, Oxford, Blackwell.

Address

Principal Officer, Accreditation and Appraisal (General, General Vocational and Vocational Team), Qualifications and Curriculum Authority (QCA), 29 Bolton Street, London W1Y 7PD, tel: 020 7509 5555, fax: 020 7509 6951, e-mail: bowdenj@qca.org.uk; info@qca.org.uk

Assessment and its uses

American actor W.C. Fields took a pragmatic view of success, saying, 'If at first you don't succeed, try, try again. Then quit. No use being a damn fool about it.' One of the traditional roles of assessment has been to determine success and failure or more profitably degrees of success and failure. But the role of assessment today is much wider than it was.

Assessment in education may be seen as a process centred on pupils' responses to educational tasks. The information relating to this is gathered, interpreted, recorded and put to use (Harlen, Gipps, Broadfoot and Nuttall, 1992).

Gathering information should be as economical as possible both in terms of financial cost and time. Interpretation is likely to involve some preconceived view of education and the particular pupils involved. This of course is not only justifiable but probably necessary. Just as when carrying out research one determines the statistics that will be used before collecting the data, so in gathering data it is necessary to be clear about the reasons. It may be to monitor the progress of pupils, to provide information about the success of the school to aid recruitment of pupils, to help certain departments of the school to perform better and so on. Recording the information too should be as economical as ingenuity can make it. Putting the information to use will be related to the reason for collecting it. If the data reveals differences in the attainment of the same pupils with different teachers the information could point to improving the functioning of the lower performing teachers. Should the information indicate differential value added in the teaching of boys and girls, this will be examined and various hypotheses for the differences tested.

In the days of the tripartite system of education when pupils' ability was seen as the key determinant of success, assessment was based on tests that sought to measure levels of ability. Social approaches to learning influenced by Russian psychologist Lev Vygotsky and American psychologist Jerome Bruner have led to a reappraisal. The concept of ability has been recast in terms of the learner's different background experience and preferred styles of learning. Consequently, there has been a move away from the monitoring of development to the monitoring of attainment. Noticeably, Office for Standards in Education (OfSTED) inspectors no longer speak of the ability of pupils but of their 'prior learning', which in turn is inferred from pupils' attainment.

Traditionally, in the United Kingdom, assessments such as tests and examinations were considered to offer measures of attainment benefiting from being objective, exact and reliable. Such assessments were used for the selection of pupils for further and higher education and for careers. Questions arose concerning the reliability, validity, fairness and purposes of traditional forms of assessment. Tensions arise between objective and open questions. On the one hand, there is the comparative reliability of objective questions coupled with the restricted nature of what they can establish. On the other hand, with more open essay type questions one has the lower reliability but the potential greater validity of what they assess. Assessment as a part of education is now more concerned with promoting learning opportunities than with sorting people into different roles for society (Brown, 1990).

Also in the 1990s and beyond, greater attention was paid to assessment in other venues than classrooms and laboratories, one example being work-based assessment. A wider range of areas of assessment was considered including practical skills, personal development and attitudes.

Standardised tests attempt to give an assessment of a child compared with others of the same age. They seek to provide information about where the individual lies in relation to the normal spread of scores found in the population of people tested when the test was standardised. Criterion-referenced tests give an indication of the actual performance of pupils against a supposedly fixed set of reference points. A common example is the driving test. National curriculum tests appear to be criterion referenced. However, they are complicated by the fact that the curriculum and therefore the assessment of it has been through changes in the 1990s and into the new millennium.

The functions of assessment may be described under various headings: formative, summative, accreditative and evaluative.

Formative assessment relates to an individual pupil and concerns ongoing learning. It provides information both to the teacher and to the pupil, which can be used to refine the pupil's learning and improve his attainment. One example of formative assessment is through the teacher's questioning to ascertain a pupil's level of understanding. This provides immediate feedback to the teacher and pupil and enables the teacher to probe and rectify misunderstandings. While formative assessment relates to individual pupils, broader judgements of several pupils who are at similar levels of attainment inform class teaching. In well-organised classrooms these judgements are economically recorded so that they can inform the planning and delivery of subsequent differentiation and classroom teaching.

Formative assessments are a form of diagnostic assessment in that they have built into them assumptions or judgements about the structure of learning. For example, assessments of reading may make judgements about phonics learning and the usual order in which aspects of reading are learned. They may make assumptions about the most common and most useful words to be learned, say in physics. So long as these reflect or inform the learning of a particular pupil, the assessments can provide useful insights and contribute to improving subsequent learning.

Summative assessment is also concerned with individual pupils. It draws together information about a pupil's level of attainment at a specified point in time, for example on leaving school. Two ways of obtaining summative assessment information have been called 'summing up' and 'checking up' (Harlen, 1991). Summing up draws together information gathered over a period of time, which may have been used originally for formative assessment. It may form a profile, although some of the information may be dated. 'Checking up' is achieved through such approaches as end of Key Stage 3 tests and external public examinations. The information provided from these is much less detailed. However, it is contemporary in that the test takes place on a particular date. A combination of the two approaches would therefore have the potential to be both up to date and detailed. Checking up should emerge from summing up in the sense that the pupil should be prepared for the 'checking up' by receiving feedback from the previous 'summing up'.

Accreditative assessment (see 'Accreditation of pupil achievement: balancing relevance and cohesiveness' in this volume) summarises what has been attained so that qualifications can be awarded and selection can be made for further and higher education and for careers. This of course relates to the 'checking up' in summative assessment. Given that the 'checking up' should relate back to the 'summing up', the accreditative assessments should be traceable back to 'summing up'. This does not necessarily imply an accreditation tail wagging a curriculum dog. However, it should mean that the work that the pupil has been pursuing, which will have been assessed formatively and summatively, should lead to the appropriate accreditation for that pupil.

Evaluative assessment, with other information, enables judgements to be made about the effectiveness of the school (or other institution). In this approach the concept and practicalities of 'value added' are important (see 'Value added: support or illumination?' in this volume).

Clearly, the different kinds of assessment will be pulled together to form a useful and manageable system in which pupils, teachers, parents and others can see the benefits. The systems of assessment should be integral to the education of the pupils so that a cycle of assessment and increasingly refined and personalised education is provided within the limitations of the size of the school. The major point of assessment should be remembered, that it should lead, through secure action planning, to improvements in the school. Another aspect of assessment (with its implications of links to teacher performance) is its increasing use in the determination of teachers' pay.

The school is advised to consider:

- ensuring that assessment information is efficiently gathered, interpreted, recorded and put to use;
- the relative strengths and weaknesses of objective and open questions;
- ensuring that the different forms of assessment fulfil their proper purposes;
- taking particular care that in the difficult areas of formative assessment, teachers are exercising the skills to achieve it (for example, effective questioning); and
- ensuring that the recording of judgements arising from the formative assessment of individual pupils informs subsequent teaching through manageable methods of recording.

References

Brown S. (1990) in Horton, T. (ed.) *Assessment Debates*, Milton Keynes, The Open University Press, pp. 5–11.

Harlen, W. (1991) 'National curriculum assessment: increasing the benefit by reducing the burden' in *Education and Change in the 1990s*, Journal of the Educational Research Network of Northern Ireland, No. 5, February, 3–19.

Harlen, W., Gipps, C., Broadfoot, P. and Nuttall, D. (1992) 'Assessment and the improvement of education' *The Curriculum Journal* 3, 3, 215–30.

Qualifications and Curriculum Authority (annually) *Assessment and reporting arrangements*, London, QCA.

Further reading

Bruner, J. (1986) *Actual Minds, Possible Worlds*, Cambridge, Mass., Harvard University Press.

Vygotsky, L. S. (1962) *Thought and Language*, Cambridge, Mass., Massachusetts Institute of Technology Press.

Vygotsky, L. S. (1978) *Mind and Society: The development of higher psychological processes*, Cambridge, Mass., Harvard University Press.

Addresses

Curriculum and Assessment Division, Qualifications and Curriculum Authority (QCA), 29 Bolton Street, London W1Y 7PD, tel: 020 7229 1234, fax: 020 7229 8526, e-mail: info@qca.org.uk

The Psychological Corporation, Harcourt Place, 32 Jamestown Road, London NW1 7BY, tel: 020 7424 4456, fax: 020 7424 4457, web-site: www.tcp-international.com

Attendance

How it can be improved

Securing the attendance of reluctant pupils is a major challenge for some schools. Hard work and tenacity are essential. It is well to remember the words of Richard Nixon, the United States president, who, whatever imperfections he may have had, spoke wisely when he said, 'A man is not finished when he is defeated. He is finished when he quits.' Schools may feel that progress is slower than they would like but they cannot quit with regard to this vital issue.

Attendance is a relatively easy feature of school life to measure and monitor and has become the subject of careful scrutiny by schools and others. Truancy, that is absence from school without the leave of a duly authorised person, damages the education of the truant, affects the wider community and wastes resources.

The Social Exclusion Unit (1999a) have outlined a series of approaches that can help reduce truancy. These include acting quickly and consistently, involving the whole school and the local community in tackling truancy and offering an alternative curriculum for pupils unlikely to achieve through General Certificate of Secondary Education (GCSE). The proposals also involve addressing pupils' numeracy and literacy problems early, using computerised registration, and offering extracurricular activities to engage pupils who may become disaffected.

It was hoped that educational reforms such as the development of the National Curriculum would improve attendance. Factors expected to improve attendance include education being relevant to modern needs and better tailored to the needs of particular groups of pupils including disaffected pupils. Also important is the role of parents and relationships between schools and employers.

A school policy on attendance should contain several essential elements (Bardsley, Costa and Walton, 1999). The formulation of the policy should take into account the current legislation and other external guidance, but each school will need to recognise its own starting point in formulating the policy. The school should gather, collate and analyse its own attendance data and should seek the views of staff, pupils, parents and governors to determine the priorities to be set. The increasing use and value of electronic systems is something that the school may wish to investigate. The school also needs to gather examples of good practice on which to draw.

There is a chicken and egg argument here because, in analysing the data, the school must be confident that the registration procedures on which much of the data depend are reliable. If different members of staff are adopting different procedures to lateness for example and this leads to different recording, the data will be unreliable. So the practice of registration must be consistent before the policy making can be effectively informed by the data. Given that this practice is accurate, the school will want to establish the apparent causes of truancy. One cause may be parents taking holidays that are not agreed by the school. Another reason may be the poor discipline of one or two teachers. Consequently, the priorities for addressing the truancy may be very different in different circumstances.

Any school seeking to improve its attendance record must first ensure that it is not inadvertently including in its unauthorised absence figures instances that are allowable as authorised absences. All the staff in the school must therefore be clear what the reasons are for authorised absence. These reasons include the following: when a pupil is prevented from attending by sickness or any unavoidable cause; when the day is exclusively set apart for religious observance by the religious body to which the parents belong; when suitable transport has not been provided and the school is not within walking distance; and when the pupil is participating in an approved public performance.

Work experience should be recorded as an approved educational activity because, although a pupil on work experience is not marked present, such pupils are not included in the figures that refer to unauthorised or authorised absence. This additional category was included in the regulations, the Education (Pupil Registration) (Amendment) Regulations 1997 No. 2624, following representations from schools that it was unfair to 'penalise' them when pupils go on educational visits.

There are other situations in which a school might reasonably grant leave. These might include study leave immediately before public examinations, absence following the death of a close member of the pupil's family and up to two weeks' authorised leave of absence for pupil family holidays taken in term time in any one year.

Given that strong procedures for accurate recording are in place, the school should ensure that its existing policies and practices encourage attendance. For example, an effective anti-bullying policy can reduce absences related to bullying. Checks on pupils after the morning and afternoon registration at each subsequent lesson will reduce post-registration absences. If there is a school council, this may be a useful forum for helping identify the loopholes in strategies for improving truancy at the same time as conveying the importance placed on attendance. The message from governors and local education authority should be clearly supportive of efforts to improve attendance.

In some areas carefully planned truancy sweeps have been carried out. These have involved police working closely with the local education authority education welfare service and schools. Legal sanctions can of course be enforced on parents who do not secure their child's attendance at school.

The effect of initiatives to improve attendance may be non-sequential and may not be immediate as the work at Don Valley School in Doncaster indicates (Johnson, 1999). Their approach to improving attendance was a part of a wider strategy to raise expectations of pupils at the school. Two strands were identified. One was to celebrate and reward achievement in the school and this included rewarding good attendance in addition to such matters as developing whole school policies for marking and homework. The other was to do with achievable standards that had the support of staff and this included punctuality as well as matters like improving behaviour during the time when pupils changed lessons.

On the specific issue of attendance, the Don Valley School developed various strategies. These included devising an attendance policy that set out what was done, when it was done and by whom. It involved developing a class register system that was available if regular staff were absent and increasing the involvement of governors, the education welfare service and others. For example a governor attendance committee was constituted which interviewed the parents of pupils who were frequently absent. A clerical assistant was appointed with particular responsibility for attendance. This included contacting the parents of persistently absent pupils on the first day of absence. The school also rewarded good attendance, and sent letters concerning attendance to parents.

Attendance is important for all schools, but it is notable that for schools under 'special measures' tackling attendance is very important (Office for Standards in Education, 1999). A report by Her Majesty's Inspectors indicated that in schools that took a successful route out of special measures one contributory factor was the promotion of positive attitudes, including those that helped to improve pupil attendance and punctuality.

In November 1999 it was announced that the government were considering giving schools the responsibility for bringing their own truants back into school. A consultation document, *Tackling Truancy* published by the Department for Education and Employment (1999b), proposed that every secondary school headteacher would receive a budget to employ staff to get pupils back into school. Because school catchment areas do not tend to correspond to the patch of the education welfare officers, a secondary school may have to deal with several education welfare officers and this is seen as leading to avoidable complications. Councils would retain responsibility for primary pupils and for pupils who have been excluded from ordinary schools.

The document proposed various steps to help reach the target of reducing truancy by one third by the year 2002. These included fining parents of pupils who persistently truant up to £5,000 and making it compulsory that they attend court hearings. There would be an annual celebration and financial awards for the fifty schools that have done the most to reduce truancy. Work-related courses would be developed for reluctant pupils who had lost the motivation to learn. These measures would supplement measures already in place, such as the use of 'learning mentors' in inner-city schools, electronic registers and swipe cards to improve registration procedures, and school-based support units for disruptive pupils. Such initiatives, if funding is suitably targeted, could make a useful contribution to the school-focused task of reducing truancy.

The school is advised to consider:

- rigorously pursuing the twin approach of tackling non-attendance directly and enriching the curriculum and extracurricular activities to make the school more relevant and appealing;
- monitoring the effect of its strategies to ensure that they are effective and that they remain so; and
- keeping up to date with government initiatives to reduce truancy and ensuring that the school benefits from any funding and other support that will help improve attendance.

References

Bardsley, K., Costa, P. and Walton, J. (1999) 'The essential elements of an effective attendance policy' in Blyth, E. and Milner, J. (1999) *Improving School Attendance*, London, Routledge.

Department for Education (1999a) *Social Inclusion: Pupil support*, London, DfEE.

—— (1999b) *Tackling Truancy*, London, DfEE.

Johnson, B. (1999) 'Raising expectations at Don Valley High School' in Blyth, E. and Milner, J. (1999) *Improving School Attendance*, London, Routledge.

Office for Standards in Education (1999) *Lessons Learned from Special Measures*, London, OfSTED.

Social Exclusion Unit (1998) *Truancy and School Exclusion* (Report by the Social Exclusion Unit), London, Cabinet Office.

Further reading

Blythe, E. and Milner, J. (1999) *Improving School Attendance*, London, Routledge.

Whitney, B. (1998) *The Complete Guide to Attendance and Absence*, London, Croner Publications.

Address

School Attendance and Disadvantaged Pupils Team, Department for Education and Employment, Sanctuary Buildings, Great Smith Street, Westminster, London SW1P 3BT, tel: 020 7925 5719, fax: 020 7925 6986, e-mail: info@dfee.gov.uk

Benchmarking
Comparing like with like?

'There is only one pretty child in the world and every mother has it,' runs the proverb, drawing attention to the reticence of anyone to recognise that what they have may be open to improvement. Benchmarking, by allowing meaningful comparisons to be drawn, enables schools to see their weaknesses and strengths.

Like many features of the management of education, the notion of benchmarking came from industry and commerce. It is easy to be cautious about such approaches, claiming that the education of pupils is more subtle than drawing comparisons between the output of different factories. But benchmarking should not be so quickly dismissed simply because the application of those principles may require adaptation and refinement in the light of experience.

Essentially, benchmarking is used to encourage schools to improve performance. It seeks to achieve this through drawing to the attention of one school the performance of other schools which are apparently similar but which are doing better. This involves the judicious use of such sources as the Autumn Package of data, the Pre Inspection Context and School Indicator (PICSI) and Performance AND Assessment Profiles (PANDAs). Of particular importance, for all its imperfections, is the free school meals band that the school occupies, which is used in determining the schools with which its performance may be compared.

Let us assume that the performance under consideration is a measure of pupil attainment, such as the percentage of pupils who get five good General Certificate of Secondary Education (GCSE) examinations. That schools differ in this outcome measure is immediately apparent from national school performance tables. A school apparently doing poorly can find a host of reasons why: the cohort of pupils and the social background being just two examples. So when schools are put together so that these factors seem to be allowed for, it is more difficult for the poorer performing school to find excuses. The more reliable and valid the means of comparison, the greater the pressure on the underperforming school to improve.

As is often the case, statistics need to be interpreted with care in deciding what features should be included so that schools can be more fairly compared with one another. Some data indicates that the higher the expenditure per pupil the worse the results. But one reason for this is that councils with the highest spending also work with the more disadvantaged pupils.

In contrast, research at the London School of Economics Centre for Educational Research by Anne West, Hazel Pennel, Tony Travers and Robert West indicates that increased spending on schools leads to higher examination results (*Times Educational Supplement*, 1999). More specifically, spending per pupil and examination and test performance were related once the poverty levels of pupils were taken into account statistically. The local authority's poverty level is a predictor of the proportion of pupils who will achieve five good GCSE examinations. The number of pupils whose families were on income support was a stronger indicator of educational disadvantage than the factor used to work out local authority cost, the Additional Educational Needs Index.

The strongest indicator of future performance is prior performance. The Value Added National Project carried out by the Schools Curriculum and Assessment Authority (SCAA) found that at least 50 per cent of the difference in performance at any key stage is accounted for in differences in attainment at the end of the previous key stage. Attainment data from the 1998 Key Stage 3 tests formed prior attainment when looking at attainment levels at Key Stage 4 in the year 2000. With the national value-added system in place, pupils' prior attainment can be used to form benchmark groups. The Qualifications and Curriculum Authority (QCA) uses prior attainment profiles in which schools are benchmarked according to the percentage of pupils reaching a certain level. It also still benchmarks against the percentage of pupils eligible for free school meals. Free school meals is the strongest indicator at school level, and prior attainment at pupil level. So it is important that schools are compared on background factors which appear to have a real influence of pupil attainments otherwise the approach falls at the first hurdle.

Equally important is that robust conclusions are drawn from the differences in performance. That pupil attainment differs when background factors that influence this are allowed for is only the starting point. The next step is to explore systematically the reasons why this might be so. When the school is aware of similar schools doing better, some of these factors can be explored to see if the most pertinent ones can be identified. This may not be as straightforward a task as it may at first appear. Features that contribute to success, such as effective leadership and particularly motivating resources say in mathematics, interrelate. This makes it difficult to separate some of the features that contribute to overall success and judge the relative contribution that each makes in order to identify and seek to replicate the most important factor.

Among possible reasons for differences in pupil attainment are the quality of teaching, the quality of learning support staff, or the quality and effective use of resources. The reasoning is that if two schools that, on the face of it, look similar in some of the factors that correlate with attainment, such as free school meals eligibility or pupil transience, then the differences must be owing to within-school factors. If the school improves or puts right the within-school constraints to better attainment then attainment will improve.

Even if this is true, the factors to be altered should be carefully assessed so that the school is not working on the wrong or less important influences. Observations of teaching and an evaluation of strengths and weaknesses will provide the baseline from which to determine improvements. As well as the direct quality of teaching, the systems that support or do not support teaching need to be examined. These include features such as the amount of non-contact/preparation time that different teachers have, the systems of planning lessons and evaluating pupil progress and the accessibility of physical resources.

All these would be examined in routine school self-improvement audits but the key point in raising attainment, where benchmarking indicates this is too low, is to identify the features which are likely to have the greatest impact. These are usually the factors that are most in need of improvement. Sometimes, some factors will be easier to improve than others. Rearranging the timetabling of the use of the computer suite is likely to be more straightforward than retraining a poorly performing teacher.

Some factors will be changeable in the short term, others in the longer term. So beginning with changes that are achievable in a short time-scale may be helpful to give the process an early momentum. Shorter-term improvement does not of course always equate with easy improvement.

Where a school knows other schools that are similar in benchmarking terms, it will be helpful to identify the best practice in the schools that are performing better. This might be a particularly skilled headteacher or a strong senior management team, or excellent resources acquired through hard-earned business links. These can give the clue to what needs to be improved in the schools that are performing less well. While broad headings of best practice can be helpful, if good schools can be visited it will give an even clearer picture of why the performance is better for example by indicating the particular ways in which the senior management team is effective.

An exciting development related to benchmarking happens to be in the area of special educational needs. In 1998, QCA developed differentiated assessment criteria for pupils working significantly below age-related expectations. These form a national basis for assessing the attainment of pupils with moderate learning difficulties (MLD), severe learning difficulties (SLD) and profound and multiple learning difficulties (PMLD) in English and mathematics below level one of the National Curriculum. Coherent pupil information was collected for the first time in 1999. Schools cannot be benchmarked on the basis of this data but the information could be used to look at the rates of pupil progress (value added). At the same time, the organisation, 'Equals', a network of practitioners who work with pupils with severe learning difficulties, developed its own assessment. It put this into use in special schools for pupils with SLD, MLD and PMLD nationwide and produced and acted upon data for target setting and benchmarking. Schools that are similar in terms of prior attainment contact 'like' schools to try to establish the reasons why one school appears to be doing better than another in a particular area. Best practice is shared in this way.

More generally, benchmarking is seen as part of the 'best value' approach. The Office for Standards in Education, for example, sees the best value strategy as involving comparing, challenging, consulting and competing. The comparing part of the approach involves the use of Performance AND Assessment (PANDA) reports and other data to provide suitable benchmarks.

Schools should:

- recognise the value and the limitations of benchmarking;
- systematically examine the possible reasons for lower performance against similar schools;
- set up a system of improvements based on an audit of the likely contributors to low attainment; and
- initiate if possible short term and longer term improvements to give momentum to the process and ensure that it continues over a sustainable period.

Reference

Times Educational Supplement (1999) 'Ministers told cash pays off in results', Friday 11 June 1999, no. 4328, p. 1.

Further reading

Office for Standards in Education (1999) *Handbook for Inspecting Secondary Schools with Guidance on Self-Evaluation*, London, The Stationery Office.

Address

School Improvement and Support team, Qualifications and Curriculum Authority (QCA), 29 Bolton Street, London W1Y 7PD, tel: 020 7243 9343, fax: 020 7243 9434, e-mail: entia@qca.org.uk

Careers education and guidance and work preparation

Attitudes to work range widely. The American poet Robert Frost took a cynical view that by working faithfully eight hours a day you may eventually get to be a boss and work twelve hours a day. A more optimistic not to say puritanical slant was taken by Thomas Carlyle who regarded work as the grand cure for all maladies and miseries that ever beset mankind.

Certainly, in the process of life-long learning, there can be few more important transitions in the formal education system as that from school to work or from school to further study. These relate importantly to a pupil's work aspirations where these ambitions are known.

It is recognised that good careers education and guidance (CEG) has several benefits, including raising aspirations and achievement, motivating pupils, building partnerships, and developing key skills particularly in Information and Communications Technology (ICT) and in communications in a more general sense. As other subjects and areas of the curriculum develop knowledge, skills and attitudes, so CEG builds the following:

- knowledge of oneself and of the opportunities available;
- skills including those of decision making, action planning, self presentation such as through curriculum vitae; and
- attitudes like self-reliance.

CEG, a statutory entitlement for all pupils in Years 9–11, includes a careers education programme based on recognised learning outcomes, careers information, work experience, guidance, and recording achievement and planning for the future.

Effective implementation of CEG in school includes the following:

- a sound school policy;
- a school development plan process which integrates with a partnership agreement agreed with the local careers service;
- managed recruitment; and
- succession planning for careers staff.

Effective implementation also involves coherent systems for recording and reporting achievement in CEG, school governors who are aware of the role of CEG and a careers governor with a clear role.

Local partnerships may include parents, governors, the careers service, local education authorities, and local networks of colleges, employers and institutions of higher education. The expertise of a wide range of organisations can be brought to bear by the well-informed school to develop partnerships of benefit to its students.

Education Business Partnerships seek to encourage and bring together activities to help young people to reach their own potential and to become well qualified and motivated so as to meet the needs of employers. Training and Enterprise Councils (TECs) were locally based independent companies with employer-led boards to encourage employer investment in skills, to nurture economic growth and to play their part in community regeneration. Among their training programmes are National Traineeships and Modern Apprenticeships. TECs were replaced in April 2001 by a National Learning and Skills Council. Business in the Community (BITC) runs an 'Aim High' campaign, which encourages businesses to work with schools and colleges and which includes curriculum development, mentoring, work experience, teacher development and management development. The Centre for Education and Industry (CEI), based at the University of Warwick, carries out research, training and consultancy in education and industry partnerships. It also provides an information service about collaboration. The Employer Scholarship Scheme links workplace and classroom and involves companies working in partnership to meet the needs of the student and the corporation. Young Enterprise gives young people the chance to set up and run their own companies while they are at school or college.

A national survey carried out by the Office for Standards in Education (OfSTED, 1998) found that only one third of careers teachers had a professional qualification in careers education and guidance and that only a half of teachers involved in the delivery of careers education and guidance had any training for the role. Good CEG is aided by a whole school approach involving the senior management team, tutors, subject teams, governors and learning support teams. In-service education and training should include planning, designing and delivering CEG programmes and working collaboratively with partners (National Association of Careers and Guidance Teachers, 1998).

It is sometimes overlooked that the role and contribution of subject staff can include recognising that each subject of the school curriculum may offer the pupil insights into the world of work. These may help form a pupil's notion of the work he or she would like to pursue or help confirm him or her in a choice that has been already partly made.

In English, insights into careers in writing emerge: journalism, copy-editing, freelance writing, magazine and newspaper publishing are just a few of the possibilities. Talks from people working in these areas or/and visits to their places of work can just as easily be seen as part of the English curriculum as the careers curriculum. They would demonstrate the relevance of the study of English to several areas of work that could motivate pupils even if their career direction was not in one of the jobs concerned.

The application of other subject areas directly or indirectly to a particular career path will tend to motivate pupils to see the relevance of the subjects. For example, mathematics is important in research psychology when using statistics, physics has a particular bearing on engineering, and so on. Talks by practitioners of such professions in which the relevance and application of school subjects, or knowledge and skills which build on school subjects, would aid the motivation of pupils who had a notion of their career path but did not sufficiently recognise the link with school.

Not all subjects and proposed careers knit together in an obvious way and in these cases, the less direct relevance of subjects may be spelt out. For some subjects, the benefit would be studying them as intrinsically useful or enjoyable.

The importance of work preparation to young people is often enormous. It provides opportunities and insights that those who have been in work for some time almost take for granted. Work experience is one aspect of work preparation. Many pupils may already hold part-time jobs, such as newspaper delivery, catering work, or shop assistance. Work experience can introduce the pupil to a new sphere of work. It reinforces the importance of punctuality and can replace overglamorised perceptions of jobs with more realistic appraisals. It may confirm the young person in the belief that the work he or she wishes to pursue is right for him or her.

Regulations came into force in September 1998 allowing 15- and 16-year-olds to drop two subjects out of science, design and technology and a modern foreign language. Schools still had to ensure that pupils followed a broad and balanced curriculum. This often translates into a pupil replacing a day per week previously spent in school with a day learning a trade at work, for example hair dressing, car mechanics and computer work.

It is important that there are suitable quality standards for work experience. The Qualifications and Curriculum Authority (QCA) have set out quality standards in *Learning from Work Experience* focusing on planning, implementing, reviewing and improving work experience programmes. Contacts with employers should be planned and systematic rather than relying on the personal contacts of one individual. Clear links should be planned and provided between the curriculum and work experience programmes.

Teachers should highlight the vocational aspects of their subjects so that pupils can see the skills and knowledge related to particular areas of work and can be motivated by the demonstrable relevance of what they are studying. The Part One General National Vocational Qualification (GNVQ) offers a broadly vocational course, while more job specific National Vocational Qualifications (NVQ) are also offered at Key Stage 4.

But work preparation is not only about work experience. Leaders of local industry and commerce may visit the school to contribute to work preparation programmes. The educational charity Understanding Industry can help organise programmes such as business skills workshops. Other relevant activities may include team building at an outward-bound centre, working on case studies say of trade union activities or courses on presentational skills. All or some of these can be organised in co-operation with locally represented companies.

The Further Education Development Agency guide a support programme for GNVQs funded by the Department for Education and Employment that is intended to help teachers in schools and sixth forms (and lecturers in colleges of further education). The support includes a helpline, teaching materials, workshops, staff development materials and conferences.

The school is advised to consider:

- seeking whole school approaches to CEG;
- seeking links between school subjects and career paths where possible to motivate students;
- designing the whole curriculum so that it incorporates work preparation; and
- ensuring that work experience is an important part of work preparation.

References

National Association of Careers and Guidance Teachers (1998) *Raising Achievement: The contribution of careers education and guidance*, Monmouth, NACGT.
Qualifications and Curriculum Authority (1999) *Learning from Work Experience*, London, QCA.
Office for Standards in Education (1998) *National Survey of Careers Education and Guidance*, London, OfSTED.

Further reading

Further Education Development Agency (1999) *Recruiting Tomorrow's Workforce: How employers can support GNVQs in schools and colleges*, London, FEDA.
National Institute for Careers Education and Counselling (1997) *Managing Careers Work in Schools*, Cambridge, NICEC.
Qualifications and Curriculum Authority (1999) *Learning Outcomes from Careers Education and Guidance*, London, QCA.

Addresses

Business in the Community (BITC), 44 Baker Street, London W1M 1DH, tel: 020 7224 1600, fax: 020 7486 1700, e-mail: educatio@bitc.org.uk   web-site: www. bitc.org.uk

The Centre for Education and Industry (CEI), University of Warwick, Coventry CV4 7AL, tel: 02476 523 909, fax: 02476 523 617, e-mail: j.m.norman@ warwick.ac.uk

Education Business Partnerships, National EBP Network, c/o SmithKline Beecham, 11 Stoke Poges Lane, Slough SL1 3NW, tel: 01753 502 370, fax: 01753 502 022.

Employer Scholarship Scheme, Qualifications and Curriculum Authority, 29 Bolton Street, London W1Y 7PD, tel: 020 7509 5324, fax: 020 7509 6666, e-mail: jonesr@qca.org.uk

GNVQ and Key Skills Helpline, Further Education Development Agency, Citadel Place, Tinworth Street, London SE11 5EH, tel: 020 7962 1066, fax: 020 7962 1258, web-site: www.feda.ac.uk

General Secretary, National Association of Careers and Guidance Teachers, Portland House, 4 Bridge Street, Usk, Gwent NP BG, tel: 01291 672 985, fax: 01291 672 090.

National Institute for Careers Education and Counselling, Sheraton House, Castle Park, Cambridge CB3 0AX, tel: 01223 460 277, fax: 01223 311 708, e-mail: enquiries@crac.org.uk   web-site: www.crac.org.uk

Young Enterprise, Peterlee House, Peterlee Road, Oxford OX4 2TZ, tel: 01865 776 845, fax: 01865 775 671, e-mail: info@young-enterprise.org.uk

Child protection
Systems and understanding

In protecting children, the school needs to have secure systems but these need to be informed by a good understanding of the issues and the complexities of what is involved. Child abuse is legally defined as the abuse of a child under the age of 18 through:

- physical injury
- emotional injury
- neglect, or
- sexual abuse.

Physical abuse involves a child being physically hurt by such means as burning or hitting, or by the administration of poisonous substances, inappropriate drugs, or alcohol. If a teacher notices evidence of physical injury without an adequate explanation, this may be the result of physical abuse.

Emotional abuse involves the child consistently experiencing a lack of love and affection or being continually threatened. Signs may include sadness, excessive crying, apathy, lack of confidence, aggression and low self-esteem.

Neglect involves carers failing to provide the child with basic needs, such as medical care or food, or simply leaving the child alone. A neglected child may appear withdrawn or miserable, may be over-aggressive, have eating or nutritional problems, or be dirty or smelly.

Sexual abuse arises when a child is exploited by an adult to meet the adult's own sexual needs. This includes sexual intercourse, fondling and exposing the child to pornographic material. Children who are sexually abused may become depressed and withdrawn, or may be aggressive, or may have developed eating problems or relationships with adults that exclude others. They may exhibit sexual behaviour inappropriate for their age (National Society for the Prevention of Cruelty to Children, 1989).

Usually carried out within the family home, child abuse is more likely to occur in disadvantaged families where one or more of the parents were themselves abused as children. Local authorities have a duty of care to investigate any suggestion of child abuse. If legal steps are considered necessary to protect a child, Orders are available for:

* child assessment
* emergency protection
* care
* supervision.

(A more detailed summary of these orders and a summary of the Children Act 1989 may be found in Farrell, 1998.)

A Child Assessment Order may be applied for under the Children Act 1989. There are certain circumstances in which an authorised person or the local authority can apply. These are when:

* there are reasonable grounds for suspicion that the child is suffering (or is likely to suffer) significant harm;
* there are not sufficient grounds to apply for an Emergency Protection Order, a Care Order or a Supervision Order;
* the people caring for the child are unwilling to co-operate.

The court has to be satisfied that it is necessary to assess the child's health, treatment or development in order to establish whether the suspicions of harm or potential harm are justified.

An Emergency Protection Order is made under the Children Act 1989 by a court if the court is satisfied that there are reasonable grounds for believing that a child is likely to suffer significant harm unless he or she is urgently moved to appropriate accommodation. Lasting for eight days, the Order may be extended for up to a further seven days. Any person, including a teacher, may apply for an Emergency Protection Order.

A Care Order placing a child under the care of the local authority may be made under the Children Act 1998. The National Society for the Prevention of Cruelty to Children (NSPCC) or a local authority may bring care proceedings through a Family Proceedings Court. When a Care Order is current, a local authority has certain rights and duties in relation to the child. These include the duty to decide where the child is placed. The court has to be satisfied that the child is out of parental control or that he or she is suffering harm or is likely to suffer harm from the care that is being given or that is likely to be given.

A Supervision Order is given by a court within the Children Act 1998 under the same conditions as a Care Order is made. The child is placed under the supervision of a probation officer or of the local social services authority. The Order may be made as a consequence of criminal proceedings and may last up to three years. There are also Education Supervision Orders.

Schools should have a designated member of staff with responsibility for co-ordination action within the school and liaising with other agencies under procedures laid down by the Area Child Protection Committee (ACPC) and the local education authority. Following local ACPC procedures, the school should expeditiously refer cases of suspected child abuse to the police or to the local social services department. Teachers and other school staff should not carry out their own investigation. In cases of child protection, these are the agencies that investigate.

The school should liaise with the various agencies involved in child protection by:

- monitoring the progress of children placed on the child protection register;
- providing reports to social services departments and to case conferences; and
- ensuring that the school is represented at child protection case conferences.

The school also has a role in contributing to the prevention of child abuse. It should teach pupils to be aware of the dangers of abuse and should help them to protect themselves and to develop responsible attitudes to adult life and parenthood.

School staff should take part in training that:

- develops understanding of the signs and symptoms of child abuse;
- familiarises them with ACPC and LEA procedures for dealing with individual cases;
- informs them about the roles and responsibilities of other agencies with whom the school liaises;
- gives advice on using the curriculum to develop preventative approaches to child protection.

Enough discussion of the issues around child protection should take place in the school so that staff have a clear understanding of their responsibilities. Staff should be aware of the signs and symptoms of abuse so that they do not miss potential signs or misinterpret innocent factors. Systems seek to ensure that suspicions are investigated by people with experience of cases of child abuse so that judgements can be as secure as possible.

Circular 9/93 (Department for Education, 1993) provides guidance on the arrangements for criminal background checks on people appointed to work with children. It sets out the circumstances in which a check should be made and emphasises the needs for sound recruitment procedures and other checks.

Circular 10/95 (Department for Education and Employment, 1995) updated and revised guidance to the education service concerning its role in helping to protect children from abuse. It pointed out that all staff should be aware of signs of abuse and should know to whom they should report concerns. Schools should have a designated member of staff responsible for co-ordinating action in the school and liaising with other agencies, including the ACPC. Schools should be aware of the child protection procedures established by the ACPC and by the local education authority. Schools should have procedures for dealing with suspected cases of abuse of pupils, including procedures to be followed if a member of staff is accused of abuse. All staff should be aware of these procedures. A member of staff with responsibility for child protection should undergo appropriate training. A senior officer in every local authority should be responsible for co-ordinating action on child protection across the authority.

This advice is reinforced in a more recent document, *Working Together to Safeguard Children: A guide to interagency working to safeguard and promote the welfare of children* (Department of Health/Home Office/ Department for Education and Employment, 1999), which also covers a much wider remit. This includes:

- describing how actions to protect children rest within the context of support to children and families;
- summarising some of the lessons from research and experience on the nature and effect of abuse and neglect and how best to operate child protection policies;
- outlining the roles and responsibilities of various agencies and practitioners;
- explaining how joint working arrangements should be agreed, implemented and reviewed through Area Child Protection Committees; and
- setting out processes to be followed when there are concerns about a child, the action to be taken to safeguard and promote the welfare of children suffering or at the risk of suffering significant harm.

The NSPCC (address below) works in England, Wales and Northern Ireland as a specialist child protection agency. It has a network of centres, teams and projects and the National Child Protection Helpline, which offers counselling and advice. The organisation provides services both to children at risk of significant harm and their families. The NSPCC has a network of child protection teams and projects working with children who have been abused and protecting children from abuse.

The school should:

- make sure that staff are clear about the different kinds of child abuse and the possible signs and symptoms;

- ensure that staff are aware of the legal framework around child abuse;
- comply with the requirement of guidance provided by government documents such as those mentioned;
- be familiar with local guidance and procedures for dealing with individual cases; and
- consider curriculum-based preventative approaches to child abuse.

References

Department for Education (1993) *Circular 9/93: Protection of Children: Disclosure of criminal background of those with access to children*, London, DFE.

Department for Education (1995) *Circular 10/95: Protecting Children from Abuse: The role of the education service*, London, DfEE.

Department of Health/ Home Office/ Department for Education and Employment (1999) *Working Together to Safeguard Children: A guide to interagency working to safeguard and promote the welfare of children*, London, DoH/HO/DfEE.

Farrell, M. (1998) *The Special Education Handbook*, London, David Fulton.

National Society for the Prevention of Cruelty to Children (1989) *Protecting Children: A guide for teachers on child abuse*, London, NSPCC.

Addresses

Child Protection Maintained Schools Team, Department for Education and Employment, Sanctuary Buildings, Great Smith Street, Westminster, London SW1P 3BT, tel: 020 7925 5328, fax: 020 7925 6000.

National Society for the Prevention of Cruelty to Children (NSPCC), National Centre, 42 Curtain Road, London EC2A 3NH, tel: 020 7825 2500, fax: 020 7825 2525, NSPCC helpline (freephone) tel: 0800 800 500.

Curriculum developments
Balancing cohesiveness and flexibility

Lord Raglan, the British field marshal, having just had his arm amputated at the battle of Waterloo, is reputed to have said, 'Do not carry away that arm until I have taken off my ring.' Such a practical response to an event that would leave most people speechless is an admirable example of stoicism. In what is mercifully a much less dramatic arena, the same practicality has to apply to developments in the curriculum.

Negative views have been expressed of curriculum developments that have occurred in the 1980s and 1990s. For example, Bloomer (1997) has criticised their determinism and prescriptiveness. Drawing on data from the Leverhulme project and elsewhere, he proposed that the prescriptive curriculum did not always have a direct effect on the practice of teachers. Teachers' values and their views of knowledge, learning, teaching and other features should also influence the process of making the curriculum. Differences in learning preferences of students did not differ along obvious 'academic' and 'vocational' lines but there were differences within as well as across the academic and vocational students. Bloomer proposed an approach to a curriculum of the future that gave sufficient emphasis to such features as the socially constructed nature of knowledge, the personal and social nature of learning and the dispositions of learners to learning.

While such criticisms raise important issues, the possible advantages of having a 'prescriptive' curriculum should not be overlooked. For example, the potential cohesiveness of courses of learning are attractive to employers who wish to be clear about what students have been taught and what they should have learned.

The role of the Qualifications and Curriculum Authority (QCA) in overseeing both academic and vocational qualifications is potentially a force for cohesiveness while at the same time allowing sufficient flexibility. Areas of QCA responsibility with potential for encouraging cohesiveness include:

- ensuring that the curriculum and qualifications of young people are of high quality, coherent and flexible;

- making sure that these qualifications contribute to improving national levels of attainment in education and training;
- developing and reviewing the National Curriculum;
- developing and implementing assessment arrangements for school-aged pupils;
- accrediting and assuring the quality assurance of externally awarded academic and vocational qualifications; and
- advising the Secretary of State on the approval of qualifications for use in wholly or mainly publicly funded programmes of education and training (except higher education).

Among the challenges of curriculum development are those concerning 14–19 education and training. From September 1996, teachers began teaching the full National Curriculum subjects for 14–19-year-olds. Subjects that had to be studied were English, mathematics, science, design and technology, a modern foreign language, information technology, physical education and religious education. Sex education was also taught and parents had the right to withdraw their child from sex education and/or religious education.

A Department for Education and Employment booklet, *Choice and Opportunity – A learning Future for 14–19 Year Olds* outlined the main points of 14–19 education. It covered areas also embraced by the White Paper published in 1996. These were as follows:

- improving the structure and standards of 14–19 qualifications;
- reviewing policies for basic skills across all stages and sectors of education;
- introducing a learning credits approach to clarify and strengthen 14–19-year-olds' entitlement to education and training;
- improving ways in which the education of 14–19-year-olds equips them for working life;
- ensuring that careers education and guidance is available for all;
- encouraging young people to value learning and personalise it;
- working with employers to strengthen the work-based route by encouraging the expansion of Modern Apprenticeships and introducing the National Traineeships by 1997; and
- ensuring that funding arrangements for schools, college and work-based learning share good practice in encouraging recruitment, retention and attainment.

The 'new' national curriculum documents published in 1999 added a new secondary subject of citizenship and had suggested guidelines on personal, social and health education. Citizenship lessons have to be taught in secondary schools from 2002. The statutory citizenship curriculum includes politics, law, economics and the media. The role of international organisations is also part of the programme. Pupils should be able to participate in debates, to explain both sides of an argument and to be involved school and community activities. Themes developed from the primary guidance include moral behaviour, the effect of one's behaviour on others and being responsible for one's actions. Other themes built on from primary school are financial awareness, self-awareness, healthy lifestyles, drugs, and tackling racism and bullying. Further secondary themes at Key Stage 3 include basic first aid, sex education, resisting peer pressure, the importance of marriage and where to go for advice and information. At Key Stage 4, themes are eating disorders, stress and depression.

Plans for a more flexible timetable for pupils aged 14–16 would allow more secondary schools to drop languages and/or design and technology so that pupils may spend more time on a favourite subject or take A levels earlier. Pupils could spend time on a second foreign language, arts, or sports. Pupils who are slipping behind could devote more time to 'basics'.

Examinations in English, mathematics and science would normally be General Certificate in Secondary Education (GCSE) while for other subjects and some optional subjects, pupils may take GCSE or GCSE (short course). In GCSE science, there are several alternatives: separate examinations in physics, chemistry and biology; a double award examination equivalent to two GCSEs that covers all three subjects; and a single award examination equivalent to one GCSE covering the three sciences less fully. There are also qualifications for students who have not reached GCSE standards. The GCSE (short course) is the equivalent of half a GCSE, and in design and technology and in modern foreign languages, pupils must take at least a short course. Every GCSE syllabus was rewritten in the year 2000 to bring them in line with the new National Curriculum. The new courses would be examined from 2003.

Vocational courses developing work-related knowledge and skills further contribute to curriculum flexibility. A qualification building on these is part one of the General National Vocational Qualification (GNVQ). Also, GNVQ foreign language units are available in French, German, or Spanish that are related to the world of work.

Work-based learning includes National Traineeships for young people who have left compulsory education. It is a route to intermediate and, in some cases, Foundation and Advanced level within the national qualifications framework. They offer opportunities to progress to Modern Apprenticeships. Information was in the form of Youth Credit briefings given to pupils at the beginning of Year 11 followed by individual interviews with a careers officer during which a pupil can work out an individual action plan.

In the year 2000, changes were made to Advanced levels, General National Vocational Qualifications (GNVQ), and Key Skills. New Advanced

Subsidiary (AS) courses were available as were new GNVQ single and part awards. New statutory arrangement for regulating external qualifications came into force and qualifications were accredited within a national framework. Qualifications were intended to improve access, promote breadth and increase participation and motivation through such means as smaller 'blocks' giving quicker feedback.

School sixth-form funding consultation considered whether the funding of sixth forms should be brought together with other 16–19 provision, consulted on the mechanism of sixth-form funding, and recommended new Learning and Skills Councils. The introduction of these Councils allows the replacement of the Further Education Funding Council and the Technical Education Councils. Changes to funding arrangements include the arrangements for the New Learning Skills Councils, funding by qualifications not per head and increased activity per student.

UCAS (University Council Admissions System) has a points system for Advanced levels, Advanced Subsidiary levels, GNVQs and key skills. An applicant profile will be developed to reflect different fields of achievement including key skills (application of number, communication and information technology). Web-based admissions criteria profiles will identify skills, characteristics and aptitudes for all programmes.

A and AS levels will be known as 'general Advanced levels'. The subject criteria were agreed between the QCA, the Awdurdod Qwricwlwm Ac Asesu/Curriculum and Assessment Authority for Wales (ACAC) and the Northern Ireland Council for Curriculum Examinations and Assessments (CCEA). The GNVQ full award at Advanced level has six compulsory units and six optional units. Normally, two compulsory units and two optional units are assessed externally. A portfolio of evidence is internally assessed and subject to standards moderation. The GNVQ single award is assessed and graded in the same way as the GNVQ full award through a combination of portfolio and external assessment. The GNVQ Part Award is similarly assessed and is designed to be equivalent to one GCE AS level.

In the North of England education conference speech (Department for Education and Employment, 2000) the Secretary of State for Education and Employment outlined intentions for increasing diversity for 14–19-year-olds. The aim was for workplace learning, a wide variety of languages, the full range of arts and sciences, early access to university courses, summer schools, mentoring schemes, more international exchanges, and using technology for the provision of a wider range of tailored programmes.

Where the complexity of the curriculum has a tendency to be perceived by pupils as fragmentary, a pastoral structure (the people, roles and procedures around pastoral care) can help pupils keep a perspective of their studies and progress. It is important that other equally valuable structures in the school work in harmony with pastoral structures or at the very least do not work against them. The same staff may have subject and pastoral responsibilities.

In deciding on or modifying the aspects of schools organisation, balance is required. Organisational structures that place particular emphasis on subject specialist teaching as the main basis of school structures may de-emphasise the pastoral structure. While groupings may be more stable in the early years of secondary school, in the later years the requirement of subject study and examination choices lead to more 'fractured' groupings for pupils. As subject specialism and choice pull in the direction of disparity and disintegration, the pastoral structure can pull in the direction of cohesiveness and integration.

What is important is that the school recognises the tensions between the cohesive and the disparate that are at work in national and school level initiatives and that it ensures that the balance is towards cohesiveness without curtailing motivating flexibility.

The school is advised to consider:

- the potential and actual tensions between academic and pastoral structures and approaches; and
- the value of the integrating effect of pastoral systems and recognising the importance of these in the life of the school

References

Bloomer, M. (1997) *Curriculum Making in Post-16 Education: The social conditions of studentship*, London, Routledge.

Department for Education and Employment (2000) *Raising Aspirations in the 21st Century*, London, DfEE.

Teacher Training Agency (1998) *National Standards for Subject Leaders*, London, TTA.

Addresses

14–19 Curriculum Section, Qualifications and Curriculum Authority (QCA), 29 Bolton Street, London W1Y 7PD, tel: 020 7509 5555, fax: 020 7509 6951, e-mail: info@qca.org.uk

Awdurdod Qwricwlwm Ac Asesu/Curriculum and Assessment Authority for Wales (ACAC), Castle Buildings, Womanby Street, Cardiff CF1 9SX, tel: 02920 375 400, fax: 02920 343 612.

Northern Ireland Council for Curriculum Examinations and Assessments (CCEA), Clarendon Dock, 29 Clarendon Road, Belfast BT1 3GB, tel: 01232 261 2000, fax: 01232 261 222.

Discipline
Improving and maintaining it

'We have to believe in free will. We have no choice', stated the Polish-born writer Isaac Bashevis Singer. Improving discipline and encouraging good behaviour in others assumes an optimistic view of human nature that allows personal growth. It also implies that if we have free will we had better exercise it with restraint and with due consideration for others. Good discipline is related to good behaviour and also to issues encompassing the following: the development of a framework that encourages good behaviour and tackles unacceptable conduct; the practicalities of ways of dealing with difficult behaviour, such as the use of pupil detention; education for pupils 'otherwise' than at school; and exclusions. It is important that there is a whole school approach and this requires a large input of time to develop and agree systems and to provide staff training and support and monitoring to ensure that the approach is secure.

The Education Act 1997 made some changes to the law on:

- school discipline policies
- detention
- education otherwise than at school
- exclusions.

In the period up to 1 September 1998, the governing bodies of all LEA schools had to agree a written statement of general principles for an overall behaviour and discipline policy (sections 2 and 3 of the Education Act 1997). The statement, which should be periodically reviewed, should include the ethos of the school, the school's moral code, positive and constructive rules of conduct; and the rewards and punishments to be fairly and consistently applied. The headteacher must draw up a school discipline policy to promote among pupils self-discipline and proper regard for authority, encourage good behaviour and respect for others, ensure pupils' standards of behaviour are acceptable, and regulate pupils' conduct. Before the headteacher draws up the policy, he or she should obtain the views of parents regarding what the discipline policy needs to cover.

Bullying is less likely in a school where there is good general discipline. Another Education Act is relevant here. Under the Education Act 1998, all schools in England should have in place measures to prevent all forms of bullying among pupils. An anti-bullying policy, staff vigilance and plenty of activities to occupy the pupils constructively are all likely to help reduce bullying although no school can be complacent or assume that they have eradicated the problem. It is important that the school is clear what its response is to bullying and that the procedures are clear to teachers, pupils and parents. The school should be unequivocal in conveying the message that bullying is wrong. In this way the pupil who is bullied is less likely to begin to consider whether he or she is doing anything that 'deserves' the bullying. The school should be careful if it adopts approaches that seek to understand the bully or to use counselling to resolve situations that it is not implicitly condoning bullying.

Returning to the Education Act 1997, section 5 gives schools the legal backing to detain pupils after a school session on disciplinary grounds. From 1 September 1998, schools had the legal authority to do so without the consent of a parent. Detentions must be reasonable and proportionate to the offence. The school must give at least 24 hours' notice to the parent before the detention takes place.

From September 1998, LEAs came under a duty to arrange a 'suitable education' for children educated otherwise than at school. LEAs should be moving towards a full-time education for every child with a clear focus on reintegration wherever possible.

Turning to the issue of seeking to avoid and reduce exclusions, a survey undertaken in 1995/96 by Her Majesty's Inspectors (HMI) is relevant. The survey was conducted for an Office for Standards in Education (OfSTED) report into exclusions from secondary schools and involved visits to 16 LEAs and 39 schools. The survey found that school practices varied considerably. Most commonly, pupils were excluded for the verbal abuse of staff, violence to other pupils, persistently breaking school rules, disruption and for criminal offences. Teachers were inadequately trained in behaviour management and many were unable to distinguish between naughty and disturbed behaviour. Pupils were referred to specialist services too late or specialist services were unable to cope because the services lacked the necessary resources. Where there is good provision, in particular where there is good teaching, there is less likely to be poor discipline whatever the socio-economic context. Schools excluding fewer pupils tended to be better at managing behaviour. The important issue is the ethos set by senior management and the ability to get a balance between school institutional needs and those of the individual disruptive pupil.

Home–school support workers are one approach that indicates a possible way to reduce the number of exclusions. A pilot study of this approach in which all the support staff were social workers was reported in a Home Office study (Vulliamy and Web, 1999). The work included the workers befriending the pupils, teaching them about anger management and seeking to improve their self-esteem and relationships with peers. The workers also gave the pupils advice on personal, social and health problems and assisted them in arranging out-of-school activities.

The government's approach to social inclusion as it relates to schools encompasses the issues already discussed. It involves schools identifying children who may be socially excluded and ensuring that multi-agency strategies are in place to help include such children. *Circular 10/99: Social Inclusion: Pupil support* (Department for Education and Employment, 1999) gives guidance including coverage of behaviour policy, detention, exclusions, registration and school attendance, disaffected pupils and working with local education authority (LEA) support staff, educational welfare officers and others. Guidance is given in *Circular 10/99* regarding pupils who may be particularly at risk of exclusion. These are as follows:

- children 'looked after' by the local authority;
- children with emotional and behavioural difficulties;
- children from families experiencing stress;
- African-Caribbean boys;
- children caring for relatives; and
- children changing school.

While ensuring that these pupils are supported as necessary, the school should be careful not to stereotype them so that lower expectations do not lead to a self-fulfilling prophecy of exclusion.

The government takes the view that there is a link between school exclusion and crime or antisocial behaviour. What also needs to be recognised however is that for some pupils, the same antisocial behaviour that leads to exclusion is that which leads to crime and more antisocial behaviour. In other words, while some pupils may be antisocial after being excluded, others are excluded because they are behaving in antisocial and perhaps criminal ways.

To try to stem the tide of exclusions as a way of responding to violent and disruptive pupils, government (through *Circular 10/99*) proposes that children at risk of permanent exclusion or criminal activity be placed on a programme of pastoral support. There is a national target to reduce exclusion and truancy by one third by the year 2002. Pupils excluded from school for more than 15 days should be given a full-time and appropriate education. Other strategies include responding to unauthorised pupil absence on the first day that it occurs and tackling bullying, racial and sexual harassment, and drug problems. The wider community should be involved in addressing truancy and a progressive set of sanctions should be in place to deal with disruptive behaviour. Any possible special educational needs should be identified and the curriculum should motivate the pupil. Schools are encouraged to develop in-school centres in which pupils at risk of exclusion can be taught for a short time and their reintegration into mainstream classes planned.

When all else fails and exclusion appears to be the only remaining option, there are structures within which exclusion takes place. The law on exclusions recognises two types of exclusion – permanent and temporary – the Education Act 1993 having put an end to indefinite exclusion. Under temporary exclusion (suspension, or fixed-term exclusion) a pupil can be excluded for a maximum of 45 days in any one school year. Permanent exclusion involves barring a pupil from the school and taking him or her off the school roll.

Only a headteacher, or a person nominated to act in his or her absence, can exclude a pupil. Exclusion may be fixed term for up to 45 days or permanent. Section 6 of the Education Act 1997 amended the law on fixed-period exclusions. From 1 September 1998, a headteacher could exclude a pupil for up to 45 school days in a school year. When a pupil is excluded for a fixed period of more than a day or two, the headteacher of the excluding school should arrange for the pupil to receive school work to do at home and to have it marked until he or she returns to school. Pupils should not remain out of school for more than fifteen days without there being a clear plan for reintegration.

At disciplinary committees, governors are expected to assess and when appropriate challenge the decision of the headteacher to exclude a pupil. At these committees, pupils can appear and parents can have legal representation. Governors should satisfy themselves that all possible strategies to improve a pupil's behaviour have been tried and have failed. If not, the pupil should be reinstated.

When a pupil is excluded, the LEA in the area where the child lives has to provide alternative full-time education. The LEA has to set out in 'Behaviour Support Plans' the circumstances in which they will arrange additional education, such as home tuition or short-term placement in a Pupil Referral Unit.

The school is advised to consider:

- developing an ethos that balances flexibility with clear boundaries for behaviour;
- developing a comprehensive range of strategies for addressing disaffection drawing on the example given above;
- monitoring the impact of the approaches; and
- putting in place strategies aimed at reducing the possibilities of exclusion.

References

Audit Commision (1999) *Missing Out*, London, Audit Commission.
Department for Education and Employment (1999) *Circular 10/99: Social Exclusion: Pupil support*.

Further reading

Berkeley, R. (1999) *Not Fitting In: Exclusions from school, a local study*, Oxford, Department of Educational Studies, University of Oxford.
Vulliamy, G. and Web, R. (1999) *Meeting Need and Challenging Crime in Partnership with Schools*, London, Home Office.

Addresses

Discipline and Exclusions Team, School Inclusion Division, Department for Education and Employment, Sanctuary Buildings, Great Smith Street, Westminster, London SW1P 3BT, tel: 020 7925 5896 or 020 7925 6329, fax: 020 7925 6986, e-mail: info@dfee.gov.uk

Information and Publications Group, Room 201, Home Office, 50 Queen Anne's Gate, London SW1H 9AT, tel: 020 7273 2084.

Kidscape, 152 Buckingham Palace Road, London, SW1W 9TR, tel: 020 7730 3300, fax: 020 7730 7081, e-mail: kidscape@dial.pipex.com

Failing schools

Lessons to be learned

'There are no gains without pains,' reflected Adlai Stevenson. Any school which has been placed under special measures or which has been found to have serious weaknesses will testify to the truth of this adage.

On 2 June 1998, the Secretary of State for Education and Employment, David Blunkett, announced measures relating to 'failing schools'. The School Standards and Framework Act 1998 gave local education authorities (LEAs) a statutory role in raising standards. A *Code of Practice for LEAs* set out the framework within which LEAs, schools and governing bodies operate. 'Failing schools' comprised those schools:

- requiring special measures;
- with 'serious weaknesses'; and
- subject to a formal warning by the LEA.

The LEAs' policy in respect of these schools is monitored as part of the Education Development Plan that each LEA has to submit to central government. EDPs covering three years (1999–2002) were approved by the Secretary of State in March 1999.

A key document is *Circular 06/99*. This sets out the procedures that governing bodies, LEAs and others should follow in connection with schools causing concern and the roles of the Office for Standards in Education (OfSTED) and the Department for Education and Employment (DfEE). The Circular, which came into effect in September 1999, outlines powers for LEAs and the Secretary of State to intervene in schools causing concern. The three categories of school are defined and the Circular describes how they would be identified. *Circular 06/99* also outlines the 'follow up' procedures intended to make sure that schools causing concern improve rapidly. It describes the LEAs' powers to intervene in schools causing concern where this is necessary to achieve improvement and the powers of the Secretary of State to intervene in schools causing concern to achieve improvement or to require closure.

Regarding a school that has been found, following an OfSTED inspection, to require special measures, the governing body, in consultation with the LEA, has to prepare an action plan to address the key issues identified by the inspectors. However, if financial delegation has been withdrawn before the school received its inspection report, the LEA has to produce the action plan liaising with the governors and school staff. If the LEA withdraws delegation after the governors' action plan has been submitted, the governing body implement the plan but the LEA assumes responsibility for personnel issues and the school budget. The action plan should have a timetable that allows the school to be removed from special measures no later than two years after the date of receipt of the inspection report.

When the governing body has produced the school action plan, the LEA has to send to the DfEE and OfSTED its own commentary and a statement of action (within ten working days). The first monitoring visit by Her Majesty's Inspectors (HMI) will take place about six months after the school was inspected. Subsequent HMI visits will normally take place each term. The LEA and the school have access to the School Improvement Grant (one of the grants in the Standards Fund) to help the school improve.

When a school has been found to have serious weaknesses, the governing body, in consultation with the LEA must draw up an action plan to address the key issues identified by the inspectors. The procedure if financial delegation has been withdrawn before the school received its inspection report, or if the LEA withdraws delegation after the governors' action plan has been submitted, is the same as for schools under special measures. The action plan should include a timetable intended to remove the causes of serious weaknesses within one year of receiving the inspection report. The LEA should also prepare a statement of action that should be submitted to Her Majesty's Chief Inspector alongside the school's action plan. Neither document is sent to the DfEE.

The LEA will formally discuss progress with the school at least once a term. Should the school not have made expected progress after six months and the LEA has not used its powers of intervention under the School Standards and Framework Act 1998, sections 16 and 17, then it should do so. If the LEA has already used its powers of intervention and the school is still not making progress, OfSTED should be invited to inspect it. HMI will inspect the school to assess progress and may place the school under special measures. About two years after their first designation, schools having serious weaknesses will be inspected by a registered inspector. If the school has made sufficient progress the report will show that it no longer has serious weaknesses. If it has not progressed sufficiently, the school will be placed under special measures.

Another procedure is followed for schools subject to a formal warning notice from the LEA under the School Standards and Framework Act 1998. Such a notice is given in certain circumstances, for example where the safety of pupils or staff of the school is threatened and where the LEA has previously informed the governing body and the headteacher and the matters have not been resolved within a reasonable period. If the governing body does not comply with the formal warning notice, the LEA may appoint additional governors to the school's governing body and suspend the school's delegated budget.

A revision of *Circular 06/99* includes advice on the new category of 'underachieving schools' which OfSTED began to identify from early 2000. It includes more detail on the Fresh Start scheme and schools with low performance.

If lessons can be learned from failing schools, they are through the strategies that have worked in successfully bringing these schools from failure back to comparative success. One aspect which such schools find helpful is the co-ordinated support offered by the LEA and others and the fact that the impact of this support has to be monitored and evaluated. It is essential in all schools that support is not just planned and delivered but that there is a procedure of monitoring and evaluation that helps ensure that the support is having the desired effect.

Another useful aspect of provision for failing schools from which all schools could learn is that of detailed planning. The tightness of the planning and the close co-ordination of the schools' actions and the actions of others is crucial to success. The skills involved in developing and administering these plans could be translated to all schools with benefit.

The Office for Standards in Education (1999) outlined their view of what could be learned from schools under special measures. The route taken by the schools that were successful in moving out of special measures had ten stages:

1. ensuring that all involved come to terms with the inspection findings;
2. celebrating pupil achievements, raising pupil self-esteem and ensuring that the school has targets for raising standards and that it monitors improvement;
3. promoting positive attitudes including improving pupil behaviour, attendance and punctuality;
4. improving the quality of teaching through setting specific learning objectives, planning the learning, organising the learning tasks and organising assessment effectively;
5. co-ordinating the overall curriculum, schemes of work and long- and medium-term plans;
6. the headteacher and senior staff providing clear leadership, monitoring and rewarding achievement, giving guidance on good teaching, using assessment results to identify where improvement is necessary and using external monitoring as appropriate;
7. ensuring that governors lead by making sure that the headteacher is effective, being involved in some of the school routine, maintaining a critical dialogue with senior staff and monitoring the action plan;

8.   ensuring the involvement of parents as volunteer helpers, as educational partners and through helping them to understand what pupils are being taught and being involved in the homework policy;
9.   using external support for training, advising and monitoring, and using published sources; and
10.   ensuring the momentum is maintained when the school comes out of special measures.

While inner-city schools are by no means synonymous with failing schools, the challenges that such schools present make them places where lessons can also be learned which may apply to all schools. The Prime Minister announced an initiative, 'Excellence in Cities', in March 1999 concerning inner-city education, with the intention of raising standards. Initiatives that were thought to contribute to this and that were already in place included Education Action Zones (EAZs).

These are local partnerships between schools, parents and businesses and are aided by private finance. Focused on areas of high disadvantage and low achievement, EAZs are encouraged to be flexible in finding solutions to raising achievement. Each received £500,000 per year from government for three years and if they are able to raise a further £250,000 from private sources, government pays an extra £250,000 itself. Challenging targets are set for the EAZ to improve academic performance and to reduce truancy and exclusions. Local education authorities (LEAs) lead most EAZs. Typically a cluster of secondary, primary and special provision, EAZs are intended to begin to redress the disadvantages of pupils in the areas they serve.

Building on these, the 'Excellence in Cities' plan was to develop school leadership, improve teaching, and improve the involvement of parents and governors. There would be better transfer arrangements between primary and secondary schools and improved provision for pupils at Key Stage 3.

Intervention would take place in both the weakest schools and in weak LEAs. Pupils would have access to learning opportunities outside the classroom and the school day such as learning mentors and learning support units. Special programmes would raise standards and extend opportunities for pupils who are 'gifted and talented' through, for example, enrichment or extension activities.

Tests framed for the top 10 per cent of pupils in the world would be introduced. Money would be available for teachers and pupils to acquire computers. There would be an increase in the number of learning centres, more specialists schools (some in inner cities), small EAZs to fit the requirements of some locations, and an expansion of the Beacon School programme (Department for Education and Employment, 1999).

The school is advised to consider:

- familiarising itself with *Circular 06/99: Schools Causing Concern*;
- being aware of and applying the lessons to be learned from failing schools, such as the benefits of detailed planning for improvement; and
- examining the effective strategies used in successful Education Action Zones.

References

Department for Education and Employment (1999) *Circular 06/99: Schools Causing Concern*, London, DfEE.

Office for Standards in Education (1999) *Lessons Learned from Special Measures*, London, OfSTED.

Further reading

Department for Education and Employment/ Department for Trade and Industry/ Standards and Effectiveness Unit (1999) *Connect for Better Schools: Schools securing the future* (CD-ROM; A4 file; library disk) DfEE/DTI/SEU.

Department for Education and Employment (1999) *Excellence in Cities*, London, DfEE.

Department for Education and Employment and the Office for Standards in Education (1999) *DfEE/OfSTED Guidance Notes on Preparing an Action Plan and a LEA Commentary and Statement of Action for a School Under Special Measures*, London, DfEE/ OfSTED.

Addresses

School Intervention Team, Department for Education and Employment, Level 2 Caxton House, 6–12 Tothill Street, London SW1H 9NA, tel: 020 7273 5844, fax: 020 7273 5780.

School Improvement Team, Office for Standards in Education, Alexandra House, 33 Kingsway, London WC2B 6SE, tel: 020 7421 6594, fax: 020 7421 6707.

School Improvement Division, Standards and Effectiveness Unit, Department for Education and Employment, sanctuary Buildings, Great Smith Street, London SW1P 3BT, public enquiry unit tel: 0870 0012345.

Standards web-site: www.standards.dfee.gov.uk

Information and communications technology

Keeping ahead

C. S. Lewis was surely correct in pointing out, 'The future is something which every one reaches at the rate of sixty minutes an hour, whatever he does, whoever he is.' However, when considering the pace of change in modern technology this does little to reduce the feeling that unless one rushes to the future at the rate of 120 minutes an hour at least, then one will be falling behind. The world of computers (including palm-tops and lap-tops), television, scanners, mobile telephones, still and video digital cameras, data projectors and interactive white boards, e-mail and the internet and the vast array of software is one in which many need guidance.

It has long been recognised (e.g. Thompson, 1994) that the easy part of developing information and communications technology (ICT) is buying and installing equipment. It is important, however, to get this part of the equation right. In order to help ensure that students achieve what is required, there are three ways of acquiring ICT equipment:

- a fully managed service
- a lease purchase
- an outright purchase.

Each has its advantages and disadvantages and equally important is the strategy for maintenance and replacement (Donnelly, 2000).

The more difficult part and the more expensive part is providing and continuing to provide the necessary in-service training to teachers and others to ensure that the equipment is fully and effectively used.

The Office for Standards in Education (1999) has raised concerns over the standards of ICT in secondary schools. Standards in the secondary curriculum in the years 1997 to 1998 that were reported in 1999 were low in half the schools that were not yet approaching the expectations of the National Curriculum. The variation in attainment was widening and the subject was the least well taught. This was related to teacher knowledge and skills.

The essential point on which to focus is the use of technology to create or enhance learning. Individualising of learning is manageable with ICT because the computer can respond to the pace at which the pupil works, the number of times a point may need to be reinforced before it is mastered, and so on. The practical use of computers is a strong motivating factor. For example, pupils using desk-top publishing software to produce a school newspaper are learning by hands-on experience. The freedom that software, such as word-processing software, allows encourages the important activities of drafting and polishing work to reach the stage of a finished product without the fear of 'getting things wrong' the first time round. Access to learning can be widened by the use of ICT, for instance through the use of talking computers for blind pupils. Higher-order skills can be developed using ICT as with computer modelling of economic forecasts and decisions to teach and develop thinking in economics terms.

A strong current of ICT developments are top-down ones encouraged by the government. Every school should have enough computers and should be connected to the internet. The annual level of spending on ICT was expected to increase from the year 1998 to 2000. Excellent software and content should be available to teachers and pupils and ICT should drive up standards. Teachers should feel confident and competent to use ICT in their teaching.

Because of the top-down nature of the approach, LEA plans and school plans need to be related to each other and to government objectives. At LEA level, LEAs were invited to prepare ICT development plans. This was as part of the programme to support the National Grid for Learning (NGfL), a web-site that has a developing infrastructure around education and learning technology. This work would translate into financial and advisory support to schools.

The NGfL will enable schools to link together, share resources and work on collaborative projects so schools should make sure that their hardware, software and any services they use relate to collaboration. A framework for implementing IT should include budgeting, staff development, planning and deployment of the IT co-ordinator.

- Budgeting would focus on hardware and software over say a four-year period.
- Staff development would involve using a variety of methods including school workshops, courses and external advice and support. Procedures for disseminating the necessary information to staff need to be clear and a practicable time schedule should be made for a four-year period.
- Planning would include reviewing schemes of work to ensure that new hardware and software continue to be related closely to curriculum activity.

- Deploying the IT co-ordinator would involve being clear about the role and job description, including how the co-ordinator will support other staff and how the co-ordinator will meet his or her own professional development needs.

The school ICT plan should, among other things, concentrate on the delivery of the curriculum, especially literacy and numeracy. More broadly, the school should not lose sight of the central goal of educating pupils and should test developments in ICT use against the criteria of whether it assists education. Does the approach raise standards and improve effectiveness? Does it help achieve other educational goals?

All subjects have an ICT statement and ICT has a programme of study, attainment targets and level descriptions. Discrete teaching of ICT is indicated at Key Stage 3. Assessment could be addressed through a portfolio assessed by the ICT co-ordinator or by working with each curriculum subject area to work out appropriate assessment tasks, which would involve two assessments. The content of Key Stage 3 could be informed by the Qualifications and Curriculum Authority schemes of work and examination board requirements may inform work at Key Stage 4.

In order to plan and monitor a school ICT programme it is necessary to be clear about the aims and objectives of the plan, the context in which it will be brought in and what it is that the school wishes to achieve. Also it is important to convey this to staff and to co-ordinate the work of staff and outside agencies in the planning process.

The school will need to carry out an audit of what technologies are used and then plan how newer technologies will relate to what is in place already. Similarly the school can audit the skills of staff and determine the training and other developments necessary to ensure that staff skills enable the fullest use to be made of the new technologies.

Project management approaches may be used to ensure progress. For example, a steering group could review progress, an action plan can indicate the major milestones and roles should be clear.

The use of ICT to aid in the management and administration of the school is constantly developing. For example, SIMS NOVA Q4-Curriculum Query Module offers a range of scheduling information: access to timetables, invigilating and cover information; facilities to allow access to summary information of cover schedules; staff meeting scheduling routines; and access to pupils' personal details including information on current location. NOVA E4-Examinations management concerns examination administration and analysis. It provides data import and export facilities to exchange information with examination boards; it gives selection for including/excluding data in analysis tables; it allows school and private candidates to be entered singly or *en bloc*; and it prints slips for entry validation by students and teaching staff.

Other developments include Options 5, a programme for the design of options systems, using information about student subject choices. MIDAS for Windows offers an overview of system information, including staff and pupil record cards. It allows a check on attendance records or time-table information for pupils or staff; it will locate staff or students at any time; and it enables the viewing of financial information. Personnel for Windows is concerned with staff records. It has facilities for automating annual increments and updating of pay awards. Value Added Analysis enables schools to compare their results with the national profile. With data from the SIMS examination module it can assess the value of value added from General Certificate of Secondary Education to Advanced level. For benchmarking, schools can compare their own result with those of a large cohort.

The school is advised to consider:

- being clear about and concentrating on the use of ICT as a means of learning and as an area of learning in itself;
- ensuring that staff training and development secures the fullest and most effective use of ICT resources both in the curriculum and in supporting school administration; and
- ensuring that teacher knowledge and skills are sufficiently high to raise standards of pupil attainment to at least expected levels.

References

Donnelly, J. (2000) *ICT and the Learning Revolution*, Leicester, Secondary Heads Association.

Office for Standards in Education (1999) *Standards in the Secondary Curriculum*, London, OfSTED.

Thompson, N. (1994) 'Computers, curriculum and the environment' in Moon, B. and Shelton Mayes, A. (1996) *Teaching and Learning in the Secondary School*, London, Routledge.

Further reading

Kerry, T. (2000) *Surviving the Future: Changing education in a changing world*, Working Paper 40, Lincoln, University of Lincolnshire and Humberside.

Addresses

The British Educational Communications and Technology Agency (BECTA), Millburn Hill Road, Science Park, Coventry CV4 7HS, tel: 01203 416 994, fax: 01203 411 994, web-site: www.becta.org.uk

National Grid for Learning (address and telephone number as for BECTA), web-site: www.dfee.gov.uk/grid/index.htm

SIMS Educational Services Ltd. (Head Office), The SIMS Centre, Stannard Way, Priory Business Park, Cardington, Bedford MK44 3SG, tel: 01234 838 080, fax: 01234 838 092, web-site: www@sims.co.uk

Virtual Teacher Centre, web-site: www.vtc.ngfl.gov.uk

Leadership and management
Its impact in the classroom

'All men are born equal, but quite a few get over it', said businessman Lord Mancroft. Among those who do, some go on to lead and manage.

A useful distinction may be made between leadership, as involving setting a vision and motivating other to follow it, and management, as implying the day-to-day arrangements within that overall vision and direction.

The leadership of the headteacher is very important but it is not the only factor in ensuring that the school is well led. When leadership and management is discussed, it is often assumed that the discussion applies to the headteacher and senior managers and perhaps to the chairperson of governors. The rest of the staff, the pupils, the remaining governors are the 'led'. By definition, whenever there is a leader there are the led, but for a school to be effective in its leadership and management the skills and knowledge involved should be much more widely based or the potential benefits are enervated. Just as to teach is to learn, to lead is to understand better how to be led. It is to understand the constraints and compromises of leadership and this is likely to encourage better support for a person who is later leading. Leadership applies to the role of the headteacher, pupils, staff and governors, and others in varying degrees and at different times.

In general, an important part of the headteacher's role is that he or she faces two ways. He or she has the inside knowledge of the school which parents and governors lack and has the outside understanding of the school which teachers and other do not possess. The potential strength of the position stems from this unique insight. Drawing on this, the headteacher has to decide upon a vision and a sense of direction for the school and determine the course to take to achieve it. The next step is for the headteacher to communicate this vision to others and through personal authority convince others that it is the right path.

The headteacher's leadership is unusual in that it involves gaining the respect and confidence of both adults and children and young people. It involves consultation as well as taking decisions alone when necessary.

The National Standards for headteachers (Teacher Training Agency, 1998) represent the knowledge, understanding, skills and attributes relating to the key areas of headship. The standards cover the core purpose of the headteacher and the key outcomes of headship. The key outcomes of headship are expressed in relation to the school, pupils, teachers, parents and governors. Skills and attributes are viewed as leadership skills, decision-making skills, communication skills, self-management and attributes such as 'personal impact and presence'. The key areas of headship are considered to be the strategic direction and development of the school, teaching and learning, leading and managing staff, the efficient and effective deployment of staff and resources, and accountability. The Headteachers' Leadership and Management Programme (HEADLAMP) offers new headteachers training in headship.

The qualification will not of course guarantee that the person who acquires it is a good headteacher but it will indicate that he or she knows what is required. This is a step nearer good headship than both not knowing what is required and not achieving it.

The National Professional Qualification for Headship (NPQH) was modified into a new programme from Autumn 2000 and became a mandatory qualification for those taking up new headship. The Leadership Programme for serving headteachers comprises pre-workshop preparation, a residential workshop, post-workshop support, and a follow-up day.

Also important are the leadership skills of the deputy headteachers and subject leaders in schools. National standards for subject leaders (Teacher Training Agency, 1998) set out the knowledge, understanding, skills and attributes relating to the key areas of subject leadership. They cover: the core purpose of the subject leader; key outcomes of subject leadership; professional knowledge and understanding; skills and attributes; and key areas of leadership. The key outcomes of subject leadership are expressed in relation to pupils, teachers, parents, headteachers and other senior managers, and other adults in the school and in the community. Skills and attributes concern leadership skills, decision-making skills, communication skills, self-management and attributes (such as confidence). Key areas of subject leadership are seen as strategic direction and development of the subject, teaching and learning, leading and managing staff, and the efficient and effective deployment of staff and resources.

An illustration of the impact of leadership and management can be seen in its effect on the management of classrooms in the school. Being at the receiving end of poor classroom management may have been one of the factors leading Mark Twain to say, 'I have never let my schooling interfere with my education.' It may have also been at the bottom of the comment by novelist Evelyn Waugh that, 'Anyone who has been to an English public school will always feel comparatively at home in prison.'

These essentials are as much the folklore of teaching as the result of systematic research. Good teachers' skills have been summarised as the ability to:

- appraise a situation and formulate moves;
- select appropriate teaching methods and materials drawing on experience; and
- act quickly and effectively.

Good interpersonal skills are also important such as awareness of non-verbal signals and conveying empathy and respect. It is helpful to give examples and to clarify and summarise (Kerry and Price, 1996). The culture and values of pupils may be different and although this may not create difficulties, it is important to be aware of differences where they are likely to inform teaching. Obvious differences between teacher and pupil include age, experience and education. Other differences may be overall intelligence, social class and cultural background.

A good teacher is able to adapt different teaching approaches to suit the content and aims of a lesson. Three main teaching processes are whole class teaching, group work and individualised learning. Among the advantages of whole class teaching are that it provides in theory at least all pupils in the class with a shared information or knowledge and experience. It allows the teacher to convey knowledge in a short time. It helps to keep pupils at a similar level to aid coverage of the curriculum. It can help ensure that all pupils cover the core aspects of course work. It can convey skills or instructions before the teacher divides the class into groups to conduct group or individual work. It allows the use of shared resources for example the use of an overhead projector and may therefore be more economical of resources. In the hands of a skilled teacher, whole class interactive teaching allows pupils to contribute and to learn actively. Group work lends itself to project work, discussion, learning skill, problem solving and active learning. It allows and encourages pupils to work co-operatively, allows pupils to learn from each other and removes the fear from some pupils of contributing to whole class discussions. It enables the teacher to circulate among the groups and assess the work of individual pupils. It encourages pupil self-reliance and encourages independence from the teacher. Individualised learning allows a pupil an opportunity to be creative. It enables tasks to be set for the pupil that are appropriate, for example, ones that draw on a personal interest. Encouraging pupils to work at their own pace, individual work allows pupils to work independently from time to time. The approach can enable teachers to assess the strengths and weaknesses of particular pupils (Kerry and Price, 1996).

Brophy (1979, 1983) provides another perspective on effective classroom management. This consists of the following:

- 'withitness', an acute awareness of all that is going on in the class-room;
- 'overlapping', being able to deal with many tasks at the same time seemingly effortlessly;
- momentum and pacing, keeping a brisk pace;
- maintaining a high level of group alertness and accountability, for example by conveying to pupils that they may be called on at any time; and
- variety and challenge in individual work.

The skills associated with successful teaching are evident in the judgements made by Office for Standards in Education (OfSTED) inspectors and outlined in the OfSTED Handbook (Office for Standards in Education, 1999). Quality of teaching is assessed according to various features. These include the extent to which teachers plan effectively, and use methods that enable all pupils to learn effectively. Also assessed is the degree to which teachers manage pupils well and insist on high standards of behaviour, and use time, support staff and other resources, especially information and communications technology, effectively.

Planning is a prerequisite to successful classroom management in that once planning is clear and conveyed to the pupils, the lesson is more likely to succeed (Kerry, 1999). Where methods and organisational strategies are successful, the pupils tend to be fully occupied on learning and this aids classroom management. The direct management of pupils is not an abstract separate feature of good lessons but stems from and relates to the other features conversant to effective learning. An indication of time and resources being used effectively is a brisk pace to lessons and the fullest use of the available resources.

In applying the skills of leadership to the issue of classroom management the headteacher and other senior staff will be able to ask themselves a series of searching questions. How do they know the standards of classroom management throughout the school? How do they know the weaknesses and strengths of classroom management? What it is that they do which contributes to improved classroom management? How do they know that any intervention or support is effective? What is the contribution of senior managers to a culture in the school which fosters good classroom management? Does training reflect the need for teachers to have a range of classroom strategies? Do training and support encourage and reward 'withitness', overlapping, pace and variety?

The school should:

- recognise the central importance of the headteacher;
- be careful not to overlook the importance of recognising and encour-

aging leadership among other adults, young people and children in the school community;

- be sure that the vision of the school and its sense of direction is clearly conveyed and that members of the school community are persuaded as far as possible of its merit;
- ensure that all teachers are clear about what constitutes good teaching;
- monitor teaching so that the weaknesses and strengths of each teacher are known and so that weaknesses can be minimised through such means as in-service training; and
- set up a range of support mechanisms to improve teaching, such as access to 'outside' courses, in-school training, lesson observations of excellent teachers and mentoring.

References

Brophy, J. E. (1979) 'Teacher behaviour and its effects' *Journal of Educational Psychology* 71, 6.

Brophy, J. E. (1983) 'Classroom organisation and management' *The Elementary School Journal* 83, 4.

Kerry, T. (1999) *Learning objectives, task setting and differentiation*, London, Hodder and Stoughton.

Kerry, T. and Price, G. (1996) 'The Classroom: Organisation, effectiveness and resources' in Farrell, M. (ed.) *Distance Education for Teaching*, Reading, Centre for British Teachers.

Office for Standards in Education (1999) *Handbook for Inspecting Secondary Schools with Guidance on Self-Evaluation*, London, The Stationery Office.

Further reading

Kerry, T. (2000) *Mastering Deputy Headship*, London, Pearson Education.

Teacher Training Agency (1998) *The National Standards for Head Teachers*, London, TTA.

Addresses

Department for Education and Employment (DfEE) Headship Information, St. Mary's Green, Tattersall Way, Chelmsford, Essex CM1 3TU, tel: 0845 716 5136, fax: 01245 492 514, e-mail: publications@ttalit.co.uk

The National Association of Headteachers, web-site: www.naht.org.uk

National College of School Leadership, University of Nottingham Jubillee Campus, University of Nottingham, Nottingham.

School leadership and management search page for education line, web-site: www.leeds.ac.uk/educal/slm.htm

The Scottish Council for Research in Education, web-site: www.scre.ac.uk/ summary/rr86.html   (a report).

The Secondary Heads Association, web-site: www.sha.org.uk

Teacher Unit, Department for Education and Employment, Sanctuary Buildings, Great Smith Street, Westminster, London SW1P 3BT, tel: 020 7925 5000, fax: 020 7925 6000.

Times Educational Supplement, web-site: www.tes.co.uk

Media relationships

Relationships between a school and the media can be fraught but with proper management can be productive too. Media often includes the local paper, radio and television networks but may from time to time involve contact with the national media.

The essence of the relationship between school and media is that the media depends on news or topical information and the school can supply information. The information that the school wishes to provide will be positive and will enhance the school's image. Certain sections of the media are more interested in scandal and tittle-tattle. There is a middle ground, however, from which both can benefit. The following might make a rather pedestrian communication.

Press release
Great Potential School today announced its examination results, which were even better than those of the previous year. Ninety per cent of pupils passed at least five good General Certificate of Education (GCSE) examinations.

But how could it be improved? A good place to start is to scrutinise the local paper and to see the sort of stories it covers. If you are to produce a press release it will improve the chances of publication if it matches the interests and style of the paper. Newspapers like topical links to present a story as news so if the school has an important anniversary, be sure that the local paper is informed well in advance. It might be the anniversary of the founding of the school or a celebration of twenty years of loyal service by a member of staff. Bearing this in mind, a better version of the above press release might be as follows.

Press Release
Friends and ex-pupils gathered on Wednesday evening 20 March to honour Mrs. Violet Trimble who announced her retirement after serving at Great Potential School for thirty years. She said she was

proud to have been part of the success story of the school's progress. Only the week before, she reminded audience in the packed hall, the school had announced its examination results, which were even better than those of the previous year. Ninty per cent of pupils passed at least five good General Certificate of Education examinations (GCSEs). She was sure the school would continue to go from strength to strength.

Another way of stimulating interest is to appeal to a wide cross-section of readers. Many readers will be parents at the school and will be interested to read a story so a school story already has appeal to an editor. But if you can add to this another link the story becomes even stronger. Perhaps a second world war hero visits the school to speak at a school assembly. This will interest many older readers who remember the war and will considerably widen the potential readership and increase the chances of an editor being interested.

As well as finding a story that will attract the widest possible interest, one should always remember that human interest is a great seller of stories. Is there a story in the school of someone overcoming hardship, or having an incredible stroke of luck? Such pegs might be used to interest editors and at the same time be the vehicle for introducing to the readers some positive information about the school.

A more indirect but important form of publicity comes when staff of the school have articles published in the professional press. This might particularly help the school in recruiting good-quality staff. If the school is known in the profession and viewed in a positive light then the likelihood of strong and plentiful applications when a post is advertised is stronger.

Contact with the press after an Office for Standards in Education (OfSTED) report has been published is a particular challenge. It is much easier of course if the report is very positive. But even if there are important areas of criticism, these can be presented to the press in a realistic yet positive light. It is especially important to make it clear in press releases that if there are criticisms, they are being vigorously addressed.

As well as the local paper, radio and television offer opportunities for presenting the school in a good light. Preparation and confidence are important. As every politician knows, you prepare the points you want to make and make these points irrespective of the questions asked. The miners' leader of the 1980s Arthur Scargill was particularly adept at answering the questions he wanted rather than the ones asked. A parody of typical exchanges would be something like:

Reporter: 'Can you be sure that the miners will hold out?'
Mr Scargill: 'I'll tell you what I can be sure of . . .'

An hour or two spent listening carefully to the answers of public figures to journalists' questions will illustrate the technique well.

A particularly difficult set of contacts with the media can emerge if the journalist has some negative piece of information about the school and contacts the school for comment. Here evasion will seem cavalier. So if a headteacher picks up the telephone to hear, 'I understand that a pupil of the school has been arrested for shoplifting. What is your comment?', it is best not to be evasive. It is legitimate to say something like, 'I do not have all the facts in front of me at the moment but perhaps I could take your number and get back to you within the hour.'

Of course, if such an undertaking is given, it is essential that the headteacher does return the call and gives a considered response to the points raised. While the school will put its own gloss on the situation, the spokesperson should remember that they are unlikely to be the only source for the story. So if a more rounded perspective can be presented, this will be beneficial. The school can indicate that there is a problem with finances and there may be a few parents who are worried or doubtful about the school's ability to set the situation straight. However, the school is confident that the situation can be sorted out. A recent visit from the auditor has confirmed this view.

The response, 'No comment', may seem like a reasonable stone-walling tactic if a reporter asks difficult questions. But such an expression can be set in a story to give a negative impression of the school: 'Parents of the school were concerned about the rumours concerning the school's future and had tried to get information from the headteacher but said they had found him uncooperative. Asked what the future of the school was the headteacher told our reporter, "No comment"'.

It is generally best to say nothing off the record. News stories appear in the national press from time to time in which there has been an apparent misunderstanding about whether comments were or were not off the record. It is probably best not to risk the confusion.

The possibility of getting a captivating photograph is likely to increase the interest of the press in a school story. This is not solely restricted to visits from well-known people, but can include pictures of an innovative piece of equipment that the school has just installed or a picture of students in attractive costumes in a school production.

Once the school has achieved good press coverage, the article can be displayed in the entrance area or at other eye-catching points around the school. It may be helpful to buy ten or so copies of the articles so that the display can be replaced every two or three months to keep it looking fresh. Yellowing articles faded by sunlight do not give the impression of a dynamic go-ahead school.

The school can make high-quality tapes, for example of a concert or of an interview with a grateful ex-pupil who has done well. These can be offered to local radio stations along with a word-processed transcript.

The *Education Year Book* (annually) lists the educational correspondents of national and local papers. The Press Complaints Commission (address below) can help if things do go wrong, for example if inaccurate information appears in the press about a school or if journalists are inappropriately approaching pupils. The Press Complaints Commision can give advice on what the school can realistically expect from newspapers when they are owed an apology or correction and can negotiate these in order to restore a school's relationship with its local paper.

The school is advised to consider:

- having a named person, usually the headteacher, who is the main contact with the media;
- seeking to manage the media to avoid being caught on the back foot; and
- developing a clear perspective about what makes a good news or feature story and being on the look out for every opportunity to present the school to the media in a positive light.

Reference

Education Year Book (annually), London, Pitman.

Address

Press Complaints Commission, 1 Salisbury Square, London EC4Y 8JB, tel: 020 7353 1248, helpline tel: 020 7353 3732, fax: 020 7353 8355, e-mail: pcc@pcc.org.uk. web-site: www.pcc.org.uk

Moral values, school ethos and pupil attitudes

High morals are prone to generate resentment as when Lord Macauley said that, 'The Puritan hated bear baiting, not because it gave pain to the bear, but because it gave pleasure to the spectators.' Quentin Crisp, the writer and former model, expressed a similar sentiment, regarding morality as expediency in a long, white dress.

But for children and young people the school is one of the places where the learning of right and wrong takes place and schools have to recognise the fact and embrace the opportunity and the challenge. In all that the school does, a moral message is conveyed. The behaviour of teachers and others carry far more weight than what they say or any exhortations given by the headteacher in assembly. Teachers are legally required under the Education Act 1996, sections 406 and 407, to make it clear that there are different views and they are forbidden to promote partisan views.

The links between moral values and the ethos of the school are best illustrated if one considers particular moral values. If we look at the moral value of fairness, we might consider in what ways the school ethos encourages or discourages this quality.

A pupil once said of the ethos of his school (to give the bowdlerised version), 'The teachers expect us to treat them like gentlemen and they treat us like dirt.' This is powerful illustration of a dictatorship rather than an ethos. An ethos encourages appropriate behaviour in part because it is reasonable but also because it is the way things are done in the establishment.

This could be extended if the school notes down some of its key moral precepts and then tries to identify the ways in which, in the day-to-day running of the school, the belief in these precepts is expressed. If one of the precepts is respect for property, how does the school deal with stealing? How clear is the message that the school regards stealing as wrong? A similar approach can be taken for other moral positions such as honesty, fairness, and so on.

The school rules should pick out and reinforce the forms of behaviour in which the school believes. The school should look carefully and critically at the types of behaviour that it rewards and punishes and consider what messages this conveys to pupils about how to behave and what 'right' and 'wrong' behaviour are.

There is a problematical mixed message in the schools displaying notices explaining to visitors that no responsibility can be accepted for their property. At one level, this is an understandable position. At another level, it implies that stealing is likely to happen and the school, while not condoning it, accepts no liability.

Ethos is a delicate phenomenon that does not always lend itself to target setting, benchmarking and much of the paraphernalia of management speak that holds sway in the present climate. Moral values arise from the school ethos like patchouli.

Other ways in which moral beliefs can be expressed are through work for local charities and those who are less fortunate in the community. Local work such as this has two benefits. First, it enables pupils to see directly the effects of their moral actions. Second, it relates to real people in the here and now, rather than potentially abstract causes such as world peace. This is not to say that world peace should be dismissed as adolescent dreaming but that world peace might begin with working with disaffected local people.

Within this fabric, the more obviously moral features of school policy are embedded; bullying, drugs, sex education and environmental issues to take only a few examples.

An area of school life that could be expected rather more formally to convey morals is religious education and collective worship. *Circular 1/94* (Department for Education, 1994) concerns the requirement that all maintained schools have to provide religious education and daily collective worship for all pupils and 'promote their moral and cultural development'. Locally agreed religious education syllabuses for county schools should reflect the main Christian tradition while taking into account the teaching and practices of other major religions. Collective worship must be broadly Christian in character. The right of parents to withdraw their child from RE and collective worship remained the same as previously. Local bodies advise on RE and collective worship and recommend new RE syllabuses. Information and inspection requirements apply to RE and collective worship.

The value-laden nature of the subject of citizenship makes it a potential source of heated debate and disagreement. Methodists have expressed concerns that school lessons in citizenship could lead to political indoctrination if politicians are allowed to determine its content (Priestly, 1999). The Methodist view is that the content should be determined in a similar way to that of the 'agreed syllabus' of religious education, where in each authority a committee of varied representatives decides content. However, the law requires, as stated earlier, that teachers make it clear that there are different views and are forbidden to promote partisan views.

Environmental awareness is a common theme in the media, from eco-warriors to awareness of industrial pollutants and their effect on food. There is a body of knowledge and understanding that can be identified under the expression and there are cross-curricular approaches that draw from other subjects of the curriculum aspects of environmental awareness.

On the subjects approach, English can contribute an awareness of food labelling and the language of advertising to convey positive impressions of products, which are not always justified. Mathematics can help indicate the proportions of pollutants and the scale of environmental disasters through representations in tables, graphs and other data. History can reveal the different attitudes to the environment in the past and in different parts of the world. Geography may indicate the resources of different countries and their place in the cycle of exploiting the resources that make direct comparison of first and third world countries and their global responsibilities difficult. Fine arts, music and dance all have messages relating to the environment.

Given that the school is doing all it can in engendering appropriate values, the issue of pupil attitudes can be informed by the school's approach. An old chestnut of a story, often told by Liverpool comedian Arthur Askey, involved a man walking past another man's house and being attacked by the resident's Alsatian. The animal leaped up on the passer-by and tore off the terrified man's cap and proceeded to eat it. The aggrieved man knocked at the dog owner's door and complained, but the owner was entirely unsympathetic and kept saying that the pedestrian must have done something to upset the dog. Eventually the complainant said to the dog owner, 'I don't like your attitude.' The dog owner replied, 'It's not my attitude, it's your 'at he chewed.'

Outside of music hall comedy, it is important that the term 'attitude' is understood. Attitudes (or value or feeling) might be difficult to define precisely but it is still possible to cite attitudes in explanations and emphasise their importance. While attitudes imply a predisposition to certain thoughts and actions, they are evidenced by the expression of those thoughts in words and by actions from which attitudes are inferred.

A useful distinction may be drawn between a pupil's attitude to learning and his attitude to school. The current interest in life-long learning illustrates this. It is seen as the learning that takes place throughout life, not just in formal educational settings but elsewhere, for example learning at home, from peers, from the media and from many other sources. So, if a pupil's attitude to school is less than positive, it will be useful to establish whether his attitude to learning, as indicated by learning that takes place in other settings and at other times, is fruitful. If it is not, there may be a difficulty with both attitudes to learning and to school. If there is, then the difficulty may be only with the learning presented in the school or with aspects of the school that accompany learning, such as the expectations and rules of the school community. It follows from this that a two-pronged approach is most effective concerning both learning and school, although in practice, of course, the two are interrelated.

Attitudes to learning in general can be fostered through valuing learning and encouraging an ethos celebrating learning while at the same time ensuring this in not undermined in informal exchanges. For example, in schools where 'swot' or 'boffin' are used as terms of abuse among pupils, this may indicate that there is an anti-learning undercurrent in the school. It may be that some pupils are not carrying their learning with sufficient grace and may need help with social skills so that they flourish as learners but do not alienate others. In any event, there should be a learning culture that is reflected both at a formal level in the school and also deeply embedded in the informal level of school life.

Cynical attitudes may be tackled in part directly by making it clear that the attitudes are incorrect or divisive or whatever is applicable. Also, they may be challenged by more constructive attitudes as cynical attitudes tend to flourish less in a countervailing ethos where positive attitudes are frequently conveyed and demonstrated.

Turning to attitudes to school, this is reflected in all aspects of school life in those aspects that make it pleasurable and stimulating to attend school. These include the companionship of others, the attractiveness of the physical environment, the catering facilities, the range and quality of physical resources, the extra stimulation gained from working in pairs or groups with others, the informal learning including the social and personal learning that takes place and other features.

The school is advised to consider:

- ensuring that its moral precepts are conveyed in day-to-day school life;
- reinforcing day-to-day moral behaviour with more formal teaching and discussion in religious and moral education;
- seeking to distinguish cynical attitudes to learning from genuine difficulties with learning expressed as negativity;
- challenging cynical attitudes that are destructive; and
- ensuring that staff routinely ask themselves what it is that the school offers that makes it worthwhile to attend rather than study at home.

References

Department for Education (1994) *Circular 1/94: Religious Education and Collective Worship*, London, DFE.
Priestly, J. (1999) *The Essence of Education*, London, Methodist Working Party.

Further reading

Qualifications and Curriculum Authority (1998) *Education for citizenship and the teaching of democracy in schools: Final Report of the Advisory Group on Citizenship and the Teaching of Democracy in Schools* [The Crick Report] London, QCA.

Addresses

National Standing Committee of Advisers, Inspectors and Consultants of Personal and Social Education (NSCOPSE), 2 Neeld Court, Joscote, Griddleton, Chippenham, Wiltshire SN14 6AD, tel: 01249 782 192, fax: 01249 782 149, e-mail: kaw32@dial.pipex.com

Personal, Social and Health Education Team, Department for Education and Employment, Sanctuary Buildings, Great Smith Street, Westminster, London SW1P 3BT, tel: 020 7925 5498, fax: 020 7925 6954.

National and local responsibilities

A new balance

Sir Ernest Benn, the British publisher, defined politics as, 'The art of looking for trouble, finding it whether it exists or not, diagnosing it incorrectly, and applying the wrong remedy.' In the case of the Labour government elected in 1997, education was seen as the 'trouble'. The diagnosis was that it had not been given sufficient priority. The remedy was to introduce a range of changes at the centre of which was the government's first policy document or White Paper, *Excellence in Schools* (Department for Education and Employment, 1997a). Time will tell whether the remedy is the right one.

The policy was to apply pressure for improvement and support for those involved in raising standards. Six principles were given the imprimatur. Education was at the heart of government; policies benefit the many; the focus would be on school standards; government would intervene in under-performing schools; there would be 'zero tolerance' of underperformance; and government would work in partnership with those committed to raising standards.

By 2002, it was proposed to provide education for all 4-year-olds whose parents wanted it, to have joint local planning of early years child care and education to meet local needs, and to have a network of ' early excellence' centres to spread good practice. There would be assessment for all children starting primary school, class sizes of thirty or under for 5-, 6- and 7-year-olds, and from September 1998 an hour per day at least given to literacy and from September 1999 a numeracy session in every primary school. There would be national guidelines and training for all primary teachers on best practice in teaching literacy and numeracy. At least four of every five 11-year-olds would reach national standards in English and mathematics.

Regarding standards and accountability, the government had plans for 2002. School performance data would show pupil progress as well as absolute levels of achievement. Each school would have its own targets to raise standards, and each local education authority (LEA) would work to an Education Development Plan agreed with the Department for

Education and Employment (DfEE) and schools to show how school standards would rise. The LEA Development Plan would cover three years subject to annual review. It would be fully operational by April 1999.

School management and leadership would have better support from LEAs; most failing schools would have been improved and the remainder either closed or given a Fresh Start; and the Office for Standards in Education (OfSTED) would have inspected many LEAs. Special educational needs would be an integral part of the wider programme for raising standards and schools would take steps to raise the achievement of ethnic minority pupils and promote racial harmony.

Another key area for government is modernising the comprehensive principle. By 2002 the aim is to have schools setting pupils according to ability as appropriate and innovative approaches to organising classes to meet the different abilities of pupils. Education action zones would provide support and development where they are most needed. There would be a network of specialist schools and better developed information and communications technology within a national strategy.

Also, there would be schools linked to the National Grid for Learning providing modern teaching and resource material, and a strategy for promoting research and development into schools. Concerning 'gifted pupils', an LEA is required to review or create a plan to show how LEA schools will help gifted children.

Regarding teaching, by 2002 there would be a requirement for all headteachers when appointed for the first time to hold a professional headship qualification. There would be national training arrangements for existing headteachers and improved college training courses for those who want to become teachers with more emphasis on English and mathematics for primary teachers and new standards which all trainees must meet before they qualify to teach.

Also, there would be new support arrangements for all newly qualified teachers in their first job, and better training for existing teachers to ensure that all use the most effective methods of teaching, especially in literacy, numeracy and information technology. There would be a new grade of Advanced Skills Teacher, better arrangements for assessing the performance of headteachers and teachers, quicker procedures for dealing with incompetent headteachers and teachers, and a new General Teaching Council.

Concerning helping pupils to achieve, by 2002 there would be more family learning schemes where parents and their children learn together. There would be a home–school contract in all schools, better information for parents about the performance of their child in their school, and greater representation for parents on school governing bodies and LEAs. Also, there would be better support in schools for pupils with behaviour problems, less need to exclude pupils and better education for those who are out of school.

There would be reduced levels of unauthorised absence from school, national guidelines for homework, and a network of after school homework centres. There would also be better school–business links, a new national framework to promote opportunities for young people to benefit from activities outside the classroom, better programmes of work-related learning, citizenship and parenting, and nutritional standards for school meals.

Regarding partnership, by 2002 there would be a new framework of foundation, community and aided schools, understood roles for school governors and for LEAs to help them to contribute positively to raising standards, and fair and transparent systems for calculating school budgets. Also, there would be more local decision-making about plans to open new schools or to change the size or character of existing schools. There would be fairer ways of offering school places to pupils, no more partial selection by academic ability, and a more positive contribution from independent schools to raising standards for all children, with improved partnership and links with schools and local communities.

This set of aspirations was added to by the publication of the special educational needs Green Paper, *Excellence for All Children* (Department for Education and Employment, 1997b).

The School Standards and Framework Bill introduced a new relationship between central and local government centred on raising standards in schools. It abolished grant-maintained status and introduced the categories of foundation, community and voluntary schools. Under the bill, local education authorities have a duty to promote high standards in schools, to reduce class sizes for infants and to provide nursery education.

The Secretary of State can suspend the powers of failing local authorities, can close failing schools and later reopen them under the Fresh Start scheme. A rather weak machinery is put in place for parental ballots to abolish grammar schools (which is unlikely to move the staus quo unless there is exceptionally strong local feeling against grammar schools). Where partial selection existed it was allowed to remain. Specialist schools could select up to 10 per cent of pupils by aptitude.

Education action zones were to be set up in deprived areas and in these zones the National Curriculum could be suspended. They were intended to act as channels for extra funding and the targeted recruitment of teachers in deprived areas.

Among its provisions, the Teaching and Higher Education Bill aimed to establish a general teaching council, a probationary year for new teachers and a compulsory national qualification for headteachers.

The government emphasis on standards was possible in a way that it would not have been in the 1980s. This is because of the OfSTED and other measures. The assumption is that where poor standards are found, closer examination of the school will reveal reasons for this, given acceptable allowances for the prior learning of the children on entry. These reasons will be identified and action taken to support the school or, if support does not work, to close it. The methods for encouraging others have included the so-called naming and shaming of schools which has received a mixed reception.

The emphasis on literacy and numeracy rests on them being access subjects and on their particular importance in the early years. Schools will need to be careful not to overemphasise literacy and numeracy at the expense of other subjects. This would undervalue other subjects. It would also underestimate the contribution of other subjects to literacy and numeracy in their content and in the further opportunity that they provide to apply literacy and numeracy skills in a meaningful context. Also, the training needed to make the approach a success will have to be of a high quality.

The constraints of a top-down approach (see also 'Curriculum developments: balancing cohesiveness and flexibility' in this volume) are clear. To the extent the approach is deterministic and prescriptive it may not always have a direct effect on the practice of teachers. Teachers' values and their views of knowledge, learning, teaching and other features should also influence practice and provision. Sufficient emphasis needs to be given to such features as the socially constructed nature of knowledge, the personal and social nature of learning and the dispositions of learners to learning.

At the same time that these government initiatives were developing, the roles of local education authorities were changing. Not everyone would agree with Simon Cameron's remark that an honest politician is one who when bought stays bought. But politicians, including local ones, vie with journalists for the lowest rating in public esteem. By association and because of image problems of their own the local education authorities (LEAs) are not always valued by the public. Yet LEAs represent an historic and deep-rooted tendency in education to engage local as well as national interests.

An LEA is defined under the Education Act 1996. In a county in England having a county council, the LEA is the county council. For a district in England that is not in a county council area, the LEA is the district council. In a London borough, the LEA is the borough council, and in the City of London, the LEA is the Common Council of the City of London. Regarding Wales, the LEA is a district council. According to the Education Act 1996, an LEA shall 'contribute towards the spiritual, moral, mental and physical development of the community by ensuring that efficient primary education, secondary education and further education are available to meet the needs of the population in their area'. The LEA shall secure that there are sufficient schools for providing primary and secondary education in their area.

An LEA may establish nursery schools, maintain nursery schools established by it and assist any nursery school not so established. It has the power to establish, maintain and assist schools at which education is provided both for children under the age of five and for older pupils. An LEA has the power to arrange the provision of primary and secondary education for pupils at non-maintained schools. LEAs shall also make provision in exceptional cases at pupil referral units or elsewhere. Exceptional cases include those in which a pupil through illness or through being excluded from school may not receive suitable education unless such arrangements are made.

In line with the approach of LEA intervention in schools in inverse proportion to the school's success, a *Code of Practice* was published (Department for Education and Employment, 1999). Section 27 of the School Standards and Framework Act 1998 had required the Secretary of State to issue such a code. A strong theme in the document is that the LEA–school relationship should focus on raising school standards. LEAs can retain funds centrally to support their role relating to schools in the areas of school improvement, access (e.g. managing the supply of school places and the authorities' capital programme), special educational provision, and strategic management. The principle of the 'constructive relationship' between LEAs and schools is based on the principles of raising standards, school self-management, intervention in inverse proportion to the school's success, partnership and co-operation, zero tolerance of underperformance, value for money, and the avoidance of bureaucracy.

Normally, the LEA would monitor the school's standards of performance and establish with each school that the governing body has set appropriate targets for improvement. It would also secure in response to requests from the school external support and guidance to help the school to work out and implement its own strategies for improving performance. In schools which are not performing as well as they should, including schools identified by OfSTED as having 'serious weaknesses' or requiring 'special measures', the LEA would be expected to intervene more vigorously.

The Code also sets out specific LEA powers and duties. These cover rights of access to the school by the LEA, issues relating to the control of school premises, school target setting, advisory services, exchanging information and consultation, the relationship between LEAs and governing bodies, and staffing matters. Also, the Code sets out the conditions under which the LEA can serve a formal warning notice on a school (for example where the safety of pupils is threatened). An LEA has powers to appoint additional governors to a school where the school has been found by OfSTED to require special measures or to have serious weaknesses or where it has failed to respond satisfactorily to an LEA formal warning notice. It has the power to suspend the school governing body's right to decide how to spend its delegated budget in certain cases, for example where governors have been guilty of 'substantial or persistent failure to comply with any requirements under the LEA's scheme for the financing of its schools'.

The White Paper *Excellence in Schools* (1997a) outlined the role of the LEA and this was further developed in the documents *Changing Partners* (Audit Commission, 1998) and the School Standards and Framework Bill 1998. A key function of the LEA is to support largely self-determining schools through partnership. It is based on gaining the trust and respect of schools and of supporting the value of education in its community. LEAs are to be held to account for their performance. Their administrative functions include:

- organising education outside school, for example units for pupils excluded from school;
- planning the supply of school places, enforcing school attendance and considering complaints and appeals from parents;
- setting overall school budgets and monitoring spending for LEA schools;
- organising services to support individual pupils such as transport, welfare services and support for special educational needs;
- supplying services such as personnel advice, training and finance advice for schools to buy if they choose; and
- co-ordinating networks and new initiatives between schools.

Government expects that LEAs will play a part in raising standards. Its new role focuses on the pressure that LEAs are supposed to exert on schools through monitoring performance. Constraints on this include the limitations of resources and the lack of power to enter schools of their own volition to 'interfere'. One possible way forward is that LEAs who are already being encouraged to work closely with other LEAs may combine to make larger regional bodies offering economies of scale.

Guidelines for Education Development Plans, which all LEAs had to have in place by April 1999, stated that authorities must negotiate Key Stage 2 and General Certificate in Secondary Education targets for every maintained school, explain how they have agreed the targets and how they propose to meet them. Councils should set challenges, identify and tackle problems, co-ordinate initiatives and disseminate good practice.

Education Development Plans cover three years and are updated annually. They should support the targets with a manageable set of priorities (five to eight perhaps) and a list of activities which will be performed to achieve them. The plans must address three areas and include significant action in seven aspects. The three areas are as follows:

- pupil standards of achievement;
- quality of teaching; and
- quality of school leadership and management.

The seven aspects are as follows:

- support for literacy and numeracy;
- underachieving groups of pupils (especially boys);
- children with special educational needs and 'gifted' pupils;
- schools causing concern;
- school self-review;
- disseminating good practice; and
- using information technology to support teaching and learning.

The proliferation of plans is a comparatively new phenomenon. Ministers' approval of LEA plans is intended to be interrelated to LEA self-review, audit and inspection. The use of action plans, along with LEA inspections and the threat of the privatisation of ineffective services, is part of the government's approach to control and influence local authorities.

LEAs' inspections conducted by Her Majesty's Inspectors focus on the extent to which LEAs can demonstrate that they fulfil legal duties, on such matters as clear policies that are having a positive impact on schools and efficient services to schools and others. Implied in all this is that LEAs monitor their services and those of schools. Where LEAs are judged not to be delivering services to an acceptable standard, central government can order the services to be rescinded to the private sector. For example, following a critical Office for Standards in Education (OfSTED) report published in May 1999, Islington LEA passed most of its services to the private sector. The framework for the inspection of LEAs (Office for Standards in Education, 1999) gives further indications of the expected role of the LEA. It organises the core functions of the LEA into four groups, reflecting the categorisation of expenditure under fair funding. The four categories are school improvement, special educational provision, access, and strategic management.

The school is advised to consider:

- keeping abreast of government policy through government documents or at least summaries provided by professional bodies and in the press;
- adapting to any changes in a phased and constructive way, bearing in mind the capacity of staff to manage change and the value of the proposed change;
- becoming familiar with the workings and personnel of the LEA;

- encouraging the LEA to adopt a policy of 'one stop' responses to queries so that, whoever answers a school's telephone call, will either deal with the issue or arrange to contact someone who will; and
- participating as appropriate in consultative groups and partnership groups with officers of the LEA and others so long as there is a clear relationship between the work and the raising of standards in school.

References

Audit Commission (1998) *Changing Partners*, London, Stationery Office.

Department for Education and Employment (1997a) *Excellence in Schools*, London, DfEE.

Department for Education and Employment (1997b) *Excellence for All Children*, London, DfEE.

Department for Education and Employment (1999) *Code of Practice on LEA–School Relations*, London, DfEE.

Office for Standards in Education (1999) *LEA Support for School Improvement*, London, OfSTED.

Further reading

Rogers, M. (2000) *What Makes a Good LEA?*, London, The Education Network.

Addresses

Council of Local Education Authorities, Eaton House, 66A Eaton Square, Westminster, London SW1W 9BH, tel: 020 7235 1200, fax: 020 7235 8458.

Department for Education and Employment, Sanctuary Buildings, Great Smith Street, Westminster, London SW1P 3BT, tel: 020 7925 5000, fax: 020 7925 6000.

Society of Education Officers, Boulton House, 17–21 Chorlton Street, Manchester M1 3HY, tel: 0161 236 5766, fax: 0161 236 6742.

Partnerships

Governors, parents and the community

Like all relationships, those between school and parents and the community (including business and industry) work best when the benefits to all are maximised and the demerits are minimised.

'Power tends to corrupt, and absolute power corrupts absolutely. Great men are almost always bad men. ... There is no worse heresy than that the office sanctifies the holder of it.' The historian Lord Acton may have been taking a black and white view of power and responsibility but his words bring a note of caution to anyone seeking responsibility and the power that goes with it.

At its most basic level the relationship between the school and its governors comes down to who holds power on particular occasions and in particular spheres of school life. If that can be agreed, then the more likely it is that the relationship will be fruitful. The most important relationship is that between the headteacher and the chairperson of the governors, and the chairperson has a sometimes tricky task of balancing the views of other governors and the ambitions of the headteacher for the school.

While desultory attempts are made to improve partnership, some progress may be made. But continuous working towards partnership (clearly defined) is more effective. The governing body should ensure that it is performing its functions and activities as efficiently as possible.

The strategic function of governors involves planning, monitoring and evaluating. Planning includes charting the development of the school and its long-term direction. Monitoring involves ensuring that the school, having agreed plans, is carrying them out. Evaluating includes judging the degree to which plans have been fulfilled and objectives met.

Using target setting, governors should identify and achieve priorities in the school. These should extend beyond what is statutorily required and, from the targets set, the values and aspirations of the school should be clear. Governors should oversee the progress of the school and evaluate this in appropriate ways, including, for example, success criteria, performance indicators and quality standards. What information would be helpful for parents to have about governors? Perhaps the school would wish to provide a brief profile of each governor with basic information, such as their age and occupation.

John Rae (1998), the former headmaster of Westminster School, intimates that at least one governor might have run a good school but that the governing body should not be overcrowded with retired headteachers. Similarly, too many retired people on the governing body can lead to too much interference by people with too much time on their hands. The general point is that a governing body is stronger if it has a variety of people from different ages and experiences who can bring varied perspectives and expertise to bear to their role and strategic thinking.

Another potential difficulty which headteachers find stressful is the relationships with particularly demanding and difficult governors. One approach to finding a way through this is to use the services of an outside consultant to seek productive ways in which governors and the headteacher can work together. A skilled facilitator can perceive the potential conflicts and undercurrents in the complex group relationships that pertain in governing bodies and can sometimes be helpful as an 'outside' person in guiding these into constructive channels.

To facilitate partnership, the roles and responsibilities of governors must be clear. Regulations issued in 1999 (Statutory Instrument 1999, number 2163) indicated some of the challenges that schools face. Under the Instrument, it is possible to remove co-opted governors who are considered by many governors to require this. There have to be two meetings, a high quorum and other safeguards. Local education authority and foundation governors may be dismissed if there are unequivocal reasons although parent and teacher governors may not be dismissed. An appointed governor dismissed for non-attendance may not be appointed in the same capacity to the same school within the next twelve months. All governing body meetings must be 'clerked'.

Members of staff including teachers are no longer eligible to be co-opted onto the governing body of their own school. Existing members who are co-opted may not vote on co-option. Staff governors may serve on any committees but may not take part when the pay and appraisal of *individual* colleagues is discussed.

At least annually, governors must review their membership, terms of reference and work rules. A committee on pupil discipline must be set up with three to five members. Also, the governing body must establish a committee on staff dismissal with three members. They must arrange for appeal or second committees of members who have not been touched by previous involvement and with no fewer members than the initial committee. In the case of pupil discipline committees, governors may agree on a pool of members to call on as necessary for individual hearings. There must be 'clerking' at the committees for staff dismissal and pupil discipline.

The clerk at full governing body meetings and at staff dismissal and pupil discipline committee meetings must not be a governor. While minutes must be taken of all committees, there is no restriction on the clerking of non-statutory committees.

Voting rights may be given to non-governors co-opted to committees. But anyone proposed as a voting co-optee must first be individually voted on by the whole governing body. A committee may not be chaired by a non-governor and governor members must be in the majority when decisions are made. No governor may be appointed as clerk to their governing body or a statutory committee. Headteachers may not be clerks in their own school.

From June 2000, nominations for the chairperson of the governing body must be made in advance and be included on the agenda. If no one has been proposed, then nominations may be made at a meeting. The chairperson may only act without instructions from the governing body when it is impossible to call a special meeting and where delay could threaten harm to the school or anyone in it. Also the action taken must be one which it would be legal to delegate.

The regulations on declaring an interest involve the concept of conflict of interest and the idea of reasonable doubt of a governor's ability to be impartial.

Parents, rather than teachers, are responsible in law for the education of their child, giving them a central place in that education. Involvement in governing bodies and in parent–teacher organisations is one facet of the parent's role, as is the right of parents to choose a school within certain parameters and the right to receive information about the school and their child's progress. The involvement of a parent in partnership with the school in the pupil's education is equally if not more important. Home–school agreements are one aspect of this. Parents are the co-educators of their children within their own capabilities and this encompasses formal arrangements, such as homework, as well as the wider influence of the ethos of learning set (or not set) in the home.

Balanced against the partnership role of parents is their role as a consumer. This applies most obviously in the independent sector where parents shop around to seek the best value for their fees. But parents of pupils in state schools are also realising that they pay for their child's education through taxes and they also want value for money. As part of the market forces driving education, parents, particularly middle-class parents, are exercising more discrimination in their choice of school. No longer is it assumed that their son or daughter will attend the nearest local secondary school. Parents are moving house to ensure that their offspring get into the best state schools. When their children are in the state schools of their choice, parents are more demanding of the quality of education provided. Partnership and consumer demand can co-exist for the most part. But from the school's point of view there is a fine line between parent partnership and unwelcome interference.

The involvement of business with schools is far reaching and includes financial support, pupil mentoring, reading volunteers, work experience placements and teacher placements. Businesses have backed specialist schools, that is language, technology, sports and arts colleges, including providing them with personnel and resources. Education Action Zones have attracted business support.

Pupil mentoring can be beneficial to a wide range of pupils, including very able pupils, disaffected pupils and pupils with special educational needs. Peer mentoring can be effective, but if the school wishes to forge links with business for some mentoring, the local education business partnerships are helpful in assisting the school to match its requirements with what is offered locally by volunteers. The focus for mentoring should be to raise confidence, raise achievement, reduce any disaffection and encourage learning. Mentoring should be a whole school strategy supported by the headteacher and senior managers, co-ordinated by a senior member of staff and backed by parents who should be kept informed. The system of mentoring should be monitored and reviewed regularly to help ensure that it is achieving its objectives. Naturally, the school will need to be aware of the benefits to the participating companies of mentoring. Among these may be linking with the school to address skill shortages, to aid the personal development of employees and perhaps linking mentoring with the school's curriculum and the company's business. As with any partnership, the school and the business need to be clear and open about their aspirations for the mentoring scheme so that misunderstandings do not develop later.

Corporate sponsorship of schools includes schemes such as the Sainsbury visual arts education packages through which the school is presented with four reproductions of educationally relevant paintings and background materials.

The benefits to a school of good community relationships include money from supporters, access to companies and other potential learning venues, a store of good will to draw on if things go wrong for a period, extra help in the school, for example from parents, and many other advantages.

The advantages to the community of good relationships with the school include an insight into the quality of what the school offers to potential employers, and a career ladder for student or parent helpers who may wish to follow teaching as a career. But there are potential disadvantages to the school of close relationships with the community. The level of scrutiny of the school is increased the more people that see inside it, organising people from outside is time consuming and may not always obviously relate to the educational aims of the school, school security may be made more difficult, and so on. So how does one maximise the benefits and reduce the disadvantages?

Partnerships that schools form with a range of people and organisations are important. The point of these partnerships needs to be clear to each party and as the nature of the partnership changes over time this needs to be acknowledged and, as necessary, adaptations made to the relationship. The strategies used by the school to maximise the benefits of the partnership should be clearly thought through and set out. Monitoring should take place to ensure that the partnership is yielding real benefits and is not being maintained for cosmetic reasons. Where such benefits are demonstrated, the incentive to sustain the partnership is increased and it is likely to continue to be successful and to improve.

The school is advised to consider:

- ensuring the governors receive proper training and are well supported;
- making sure that governors are aware of the relevance of recent statutory instruments;
- being particularly clear about the strategic role of governors;
- taking particular care that the relationship between the chairperson of governors and the headteacher is sound;
- ensuring that governors clearly understand their responsibilities and take active steps to fulfil them;
- monitoring the effect on the standards of pupil attainment of involvement with parents and the community including business and industry; and
- recognising the rights of parents for a special place in their relationships with the school as the parent is the person responsible for the child's education.

References

Statutory Instrument 1999, number 2163.
Department for Education and Employment (1999) *Consultation Document on Governors' Regulations*, London, DfEE.
Rae, J. (1998) *Letters to Parents*, London, HarperCollins.

Further reading

Gann, N. (1998) *Improving School Governance: How better governors make better schools*, London, Falmer Press.
Sallis, J. (1999) *Managing Better with Governors*, London, Financial Times Management.

Addresses

Arts and Business, Nutmeg House, 60 Gainsford Street, Butler's Wharf, London SE1 2NY, tel: 020 7378 8143, web-site: www.AandB.org.uk

Arts Council of England, 14 Great Peter Street, London SW1 3NQ, tel: 020 7973 0100, web-site: www.artscouncil.org.uk

National Governors Council, Glebe House, Church Street, Crediton, Devon EX17 2AF, tel: 01363 774 377, fax: 01363 776 007.

School Framework and Governance Division, Department for Education and Employment, Sanctuary Buildings, Great Smith Street, Westminster, London SW1P 3BT (Community Schools, tel: 020 7925 5592/6336, fax: 020 7925 6374; Voluntary and Foundation Schools, tel: 01325 391 100/184, fax: 01325 391 184), web-site: www.dfee.gov.uk/governor/governor.htm

Personal, social and health education

A communal approach

In a variation of Dr Johnson's famous dictum, 'When a man is tired of London he is tired of life', the financier A. E. Filene stated, 'When a man's education is finished, he is finished.' Filene's statement is as true of personal, social and health education (PSHE) as any other facet of education for it is centrally to do with learning about oneself and one's place in the world.

It is a rueful observation of those with responsibility for planning and delivering a coherent curriculum that the remit and the design of the curriculum frequently change to reflect the changing views of society about what is valuable and the views of potential employers as to what is useful. Similarly, notions of what is relevant and indeed what is acceptable in PSHE change over time. It is important therefore that the boundaries and content of PSHE are agreed in the school and elsewhere and that they are widely accepted and understood by teachers and other staff, parents and the wider community. One way of helping to ensure this is to make the enterprise, as far as is practicable, a communal one.

However, it is also important that schools are consistent within the values and ethos they endorse. Classroom activity in PSHE is likely to be more effective when reinforced in the wider school context. For example, if PSHE is based in part on developing self-esteem and respect for oneself and others, then this could be encouraged in the way that people relate to each other throughout the school – staff to staff, staff to pupils, pupils to pupils, and so on.

A school's approach to PSHE draws on the commitment of the head-teacher and the senior management team. The development of a PSHE policy is likely to involve governors, parents, staff, pupils, community representatives and others as necessary and the use of visitors and outside agencies in the delivery of courses. It will also include the role of a PSHE co-ordinator, the training of staff in the delivery of the courses, and the purchase of suitable resources. PSHE works best when it is valued and seen as relevant to the school's objectives by all who are involved.

Ethos and values that underpin the PSHE curriculum can be reinforced throughout the curriculum. PSHE should be based on sound educational processes (knowing, understanding and doing). It can help schools to achieve their own objectives relating to educational attainment, for example confident pupils with high self-esteem will tend to learn better. PSHE might require learning strategies which are participative and facilitative rather than didactic. Facilitative/group work that is person centred appears to be more effective in relation to PSHE than traditional strategies, such as information giving and 'shock-horror' tactics.

The headteacher and senior managers need to be wholeheartedly committed to the approach adopted in the school. It is important that the headteacher guides as well as consults, for PSHE should be not only educationally and socially sound but also politically defensible. To help ensure that the approach is politically sound, wide consultation needs to take place and evidence of this documented and used in decision making. It is a positive sign if parents feel that their views are understood and, as far as is practicable, taken into account. Members of the wider community, including potential employers, will also have views and can make valuable contributions. There is a need to consider the morality of the day, different cultures, central and local government policy, DfEE guidance and other factors. Generally, a system that uses educational approaches for which there is evidence of effectiveness and that follows good practice guidance which is current nationally is likely to gain support.

Personal education relates to the individual's personal development and may include areas such as emotional and personal development including self-esteem, adolescence, relationships and communicating effectively. The development of personal skills such as decision making and problem solving are important. These skills are the ones that drive sound choices and are transferable to other areas of the curriculum. PSHE draws on developmental psychology in which local education authority or other psychologists may make helpful inputs, and practical communication skills in which specialists in the community as well as teachers will have expertise. PSHE also draws on good educational practice.

Social education concerns the concept of citizenship, economic awareness and environmental education. These centre around the rights of an individual as balanced against the responsibilities of the individual to the community and society in which he or she lives. It may include consideration of the influence of friends and family and the wider community, ethnic diversity, ability and disability, loss, prejudice, parenting skills and employment issues. Within this framework, issues such as bullying may be addressed. Sex education and sexual health is taught as part of the education about human relationships. PSHE gives the opportunity to explore concepts such as discrimination, equity, justice, and so on. The spiral nature of the PSHE curriculum introduces concepts, ideas and knowledge at appropriate stages in the development of pupils. Opportunities for cross-curricular work can also be explored such as concepts of discrimination in history and English, the use of core skills across the whole curriculum, and the use of social and health related data in mathematics and geography.

These areas can draw on a wide range of experience and knowledge in the community both in helping frame the approach and in delivering some aspects of it. Among those with views on citizenship will be local magistrates, charities, the police service and others. Local employers, financial specialists such as bank or insurance workers may contribute to views on economic awareness.

Environmental education could include contributions from political groups such as Friends of the Earth as well as environment specialists working in a local authority. Members of different ethnic groups may contribute to the planning and delivery of issues around ethnic diversity. Matters to do with disability and ability will benefit from the contributions of disabled people. Loss will include separation and bereavement and there are specialist organisations which develop support in these areas.

Parenting skills may be further developed and encouraged in the community by helpful materials and discussion groups. Employment issues will benefit from contributions from employers and careers specialists. Approaches to bullying are among the most difficult and potentially the most contentious. Charities such as Kidscape can offer advice and resources. Sex education and sexual health is again potentially contentious and careful consultation has to both take place and be seen to take place.

While the contribution of outside speakers can be important, it needs to be part of a planned curriculum. There is a danger that schools will use outside speakers for 'one off' talks that teachers feel uncomfortable with such as sexual health and drug use. If PSHE is based on sound educational processes, outside speakers are more likely to be regarded as a resource that is appropriate to use within a particular part of the process. The effectiveness of outside speakers is enhanced if there is a purpose to their involvement that is consistent with the aims of well-defined learning outcomes.

Health education focuses on positive health such as healthy eating and matters that can damage or impair health should arise within this context. Alcohol, tobacco and medication as well as the illegal drugs are therefore within the remit of health education in the secondary school. Other health issues include human immunodeficiency virus (HIV) and acquired immune deficiency syndrome (AIDS). Some health education is statutory (sexual health and drug misuse).

The approach recommended by the DfEE is one that integrates individual topics into a well-developed PSHE programme with themes related to such matters as self-esteem. Curriculum learning needs are to be reinforced within the wider school environment. For example, nutrition learning can be reinforced by healthy food being available within the school and issues of food poverty explored in the classroom can be reinforced through the provision of breakfast clubs. Smoking education can be effectively sabotaged by clouds of tobacco smoke emanating from classrooms or by a less serious response to the use of tobacco by pupils than to their use of other drugs.

The role of a PSHE co-ordinator is important as a facilitator to the wide range of contributions both to policy and to provision. One of the roles will be to arrange and contribute to the training of school staff in the delivery of the courses. This could involve the bringing in of outside advice and expertise which can be 'cascaded' to pupils. There is certainly a balance to be struck between bringing in outside experience and having the teachers in the school who know the pupils personally making a major contribution.

The purchase of suitable resources is also likely to come within the remit of the PSHE co-ordinator's role. Where people from outside agencies contribute, particularly if this is without charge, they may bring their own resources and make free resources available to the school, saving school costs. Health Promotion Services can be a valuable resource to schools, providing support materials, training and facilitating links with other services.

The school is advised to consider:

- developing a comprehensive policy of personal, social and health education consulting as appropriate;
- drawing on the expertise of the community both to discuss and agree approaches and to provide support as necessary within a clear educationally sound framework;
- having a clear written policy and a coherent and credible position regarding illegal drugs, alcohol and smoking; and
- planning the necessary staff training, contact with external agencies, purchasing of resources and other aspects necessary for effective provision.

Reference

Department for Education and Employment (1999) *Preparing Young People for Adult Life: A Report by the National Advisory Group on Personal, Social and Health Education*, London, DfEE.

Further reading

Qualifications and Curriculum Authority (2000) *Education 3–16 National Curriculum Review Consultation: A framework for personal, social and health education (PSHE) and citizenship at key stages 1 to 4*, London, QCA.

Addresses

Standing Conference on Drug Abuse, 32–36 Loman Street, London SE1 0EE, tel: 020 7928 9500, fax: 020 7928 3343, e-mail: info@scoda.demon.co.uk

The Teachers' Advisory Council on Alcohol and Drugs Education (TACADE), 1 Hulme Place, The Crescent, Salford, Greater Manchester M5 4QA, tel: 0161 745 8925, fax: 0161 745 8923, e-mail: ho@tacade.demon.uk   web-site: www. tacade.com

Professional development
Towards a systematic approach

To misquote Mrs Beaton's famous advice, first catch your staff, then retain them. Against a background of teacher shortages, recruitment is increasingly competitive. Often there is a self-fulfilling function whereby a successful school which may not need the new staff member as desperately as a less successful one finds it easier to recruit on the back of its positive reputation.

A five-yearly government review of the Teacher Training Agency (TTA) concluded in 1999 that the TTA should concentrate on teacher supply and recruitment and on initial teacher training. The TTA works closely with the Teachers Unit at the Department for Education and Employment (DfEE) to carry forward the aims of the Green Paper *Teachers Meeting the Challenge of Change* (Department for Education and Employment, 1998a). The DfEE took over work previously carried out by the TTA on teachers' professional development and headteacher qualification. The TTA continued its role to find and allocate places for initial teacher training.

Retaining teachers in their first year is important particularly if the teacher develops and offers the school good service for some years afterwards. From September 1999, in line with the Government White Paper *Excellence in Schools* (Department for Education and Employment, 1998b) and the Teaching and Higher Education Act 1998, new statutory arrangements covered the induction period for all newly qualified teachers (NQTs). Requirements cover:

- which schools are allowed to employ NQTs;
- conditions of the period of induction;
- induction standards;
- monitoring, assessment and support; and
- the roles and responsibilities of the people involved.

Unhappiness according to Edward de Bono is the difference between our talents and our expectations. If this is so, then clearer expectations of teachers and headteachers and better matching of their talents to the requirements of the work might lead to better morale as they become more able to bridge the gap between hopes and aspirations.

The Teacher Training Agency framework for continuing professional development aims to determine clear expectations of teachers, involves targets for professional development and career development, seeks to improve training and staff development, and recognises the expertise of effective school teachers. National standards have been set out for Qualified Teacher Status (QTS), special educational needs co-ordinators, subject leaders and headteachers. These follow a common structure covering: core purpose, key outcomes, professional knowledge and understanding, skills and attributes and key areas. The key areas are to do with strategic direction and development, teaching and learning, leading and managing staff, the efficient and effective deployment of staff and resources, and, in the case of headteachers, accountability.

A key document describing developments in initial teacher training was DfEE *Circular 10/97* (Department for Education and Employment, 1997). This Circular provided criteria that all courses of initial teacher training had to meet. The criteria gave the standards of knowledge, understanding and skills that all trainees must demonstrate in order to complete a course of initial teacher training and be eligible for QTS. *Circular 10/97* is superseded by *Circular 4/98* (Department for Education and Employment, 1998c).

Requirements for all courses of initial teacher training which came into force on 1 September 1998 concerned the following:

- minimum trainee entry and selection requirements covering general requirements and those specific to postgraduate courses and undergraduate courses;
- course length and coverage, concerning the types of course and the length of postgraduate courses;
- partnership requirements (such as the time to be spent in schools); and
- quality assurance requirements.

Similar requirements apply to employment-based routes to teaching.

An initial teacher-training national curriculum was developed for the secondary phase and the national curriculum for information and communications technology subject teaching was introduced with statutory force from September 1998.

Standards for the award of QTS have been published (Teacher Training Agency, 1998a). The TTA standards apply to all trainees seeking QTS who were assessed from May 1998. To be successful, candidates on ITT courses must achieve all the QTS standards. Courses must assess all trainees against all the standards set out in the awards of QTS.

The standards fall into four broad headings. The first is knowledge and understanding that includes standards for secondary specialist subjects. The second heading is planning, teaching and class management. This includes standards for primary and secondary planning and teaching and class management. Regarding planning those to be awarded QTS must, for example, 'plan their teaching to achieve progress in pupils' learning through identifying clear teaching objectives and content appropriate to the subject matter and the pupils being taught, and specify how these will be taught and assessed' (Teacher Training Agency, 1998a).

Concerning teaching and class management, those to be awarded QTS must demonstrate that they, for example, 'monitor and intervene when teaching to ensure sound learning and discipline'. The third heading is monitoring, assessment, recording, reporting and accountability. It specifies standards which all those to be awarded QTS must demonstrate when assessed in each subject that they have been trained to teach. An example of the requirements within this heading is that those to be awarded QTS must 'assess how well learning objectives have been achieved and use this assessment to improve specific aspects of teaching'. The final heading concerns other professional requirements. Under this, for example, those to be awarded QTS must be aware of the role and purpose of school governing bodies.

An important feature of the Standards for the award of QTS is that they form a basis for future professional development. These include development through links with the other standards in the professional framework for subject leaders (Teacher Training Agency, 1998b) and head-teachers. Standards for teacher induction and for advanced skills teachers began to be developed in 1998. Of particular relevance is the Career Entry Profile, providing a basis for support and monitoring during the induction year.

Secondary partnership is an important thread of initial teacher training. Certain school roles are associated with secondary partnership. A 'host class teacher' is the teacher to whose class the trainee is assigned. A 'lead mentor' is a teacher in a partnership school responsible for co-ordinating the work of the mentors in the school. The 'mentor' is a school-based ITT tutor, that is the teacher with first line responsibility for the training of a trainee in the school. Other roles relate to staff of the higher education institution. A 'link tutor' is the person responsible for relationships with a cluster of schools in the partnership. A 'subject tutor' is responsible for co-ordinating the work of mentors in a particular subject across the whole partnership. A 'programme co-ordinator' is the member of staff responsible for organising the partnership's ITT course.

The 1998 Green Paper *Teachers Meeting the Challenge of Change* set out proposals for a threshold leading to performance related pay. Annual appraisal would apply to all teachers who would be set individual targets and the appraisal would be linked to increases in pay. There would be a fast track scheme for young teachers and a new leadership scale for advanced skills teachers and senior staff. Headteachers would have the opportunity to take fixed-term contracts with high financial rewards. A School Performance Award Scheme would identify the best schools who would receive bonuses to be allocated to staff. Trainee teachers would be tested in numeracy and possibly literacy and information technology. The training of supply teachers would be reviewed. Teachers would be under a contractual duty to keep up to date professionally. Many more class room assistants would be employed. Headteachers would be subject to performance related pay and there would be a three-stage programme of training comprising qualification, induction, and extension. A new college for school leadership and a new inspection programme for teacher training providers would be initiated.

The strongest thread running through recent developments relating to teacher and headteacher professional development and training is that of standards. This reflects the focus on standards achieved by pupils and perhaps it is inevitable that a similar attention is given to the standards reached by teachers in various roles and by headteachers. Particularly when appraisal will take into account these standards and when appraisal will affect the amount earned by teachers and headteachers, it is important to be clear and vigilant that the basis of the standards is widely agreed and is robust. 'Everyone complains of his memory,' stated the French writer the Duc de la Rochefoucauld, 'but no one complains of his judgement'. In appraisal, participants may be loath to consider the precariousness of their judgements. It is important therefore that judgements involved in appraisal are based on evidence that is clearly understood by those appraising and those being appraised.

Other important forces for professional development are the General Teaching Council (GTC) and the College of Teachers (formerly the College of Preceptors). The GTC, set up in the year 2000, maintains a register of qualified teachers, awards or removes the right to teach, and advises on professional issues, such as entry standards, recruitment, training and professional development. It has an advisory role regarding initial teacher training. Its membership comprises elected teachers, teachers appointed by the main teaching unions, members appointed by 'representative bodies' and members appointed by the Secretary of State.

The College of Teachers is an independent body, working alongside the GTC, which aims to assert the intellectual authority, leadership and professional excellence of teachers. Subject associations and schools may take out institutional membership and individual membership is open to teachers.

In 1999, following a five-yearly review of the Teacher Training Agency (TTA), it was decided that the DfEE Teacher Unit would take over the TTA's previous work on teachers' professional development and headteacher qualifications. The headteacher work was to become part of the remit of the new National College for School Leadership (overseen by the DfEE). The Teacher Unit also takes forward the individual learning accounts used by teachers for their ongoing professional development and the new appraisal system and assessment for teachers to reach the higher pay scale. It is also involved in the accelerated promotion scheme for potential headteachers and developed the fast-track graduate recruitment programme.

Guidance was published (Department for Education and Employment, 1999a) to help governing bodies fulfil their statutory duty concerning pay and performance. From September 1999, governing bodies of every school should agree and review performance objectives for their headteachers and deputy headteachers in relation to school leadership and management and to the progress of pupils. Also in 1999, a consultation document of performance management with regard to teachers was published (Department for Education and Employment, 1999b). It outlined a framework for performance management which the government planned to put into place by September 2000.

Schools should be aware of:

- statutory requirements when planning to employ NQTs;
- the national standards for qualified teacher status, special educational needs co-ordinators, subject leaders and headteachers;
- the standards for the award of QTS;
- the standards for teacher induction and for advanced skills teachers;
- the Career Entry Profile which gives a basis for support and monitoring during the induction year;
- the potential advantages to the school of secondary partnership in initial teacher training;
- the importance of securing sound arrangements for the appraisal of teachers and the headteacher as outlined in the Green Paper *Teachers Meeting the Challenge of Change*;
- the advantages of developing a system of appraisal which draws on information which already exists in the school; and
- the duty to set performance agreement for headteachers and deputy headteachers.

References

Department for Education and Employment (1997) *Circular 10/97 Teaching: High status, high standards: Requirements for courses of initial teacher training*, London, DfEE.

Department for Education and Employment (1998a) *Teachers Meeting the Challenge of Change*, London, DfEE.

Department for Education and Employment (1998b) *Excellence for All Schools*, London, DfEE.

Department for Education and Employment (1998c) *Circular 4/98, Teaching: High status, high standards: requirements for courses of initial teacher training*, London, DfEE.

Department for Education and Employment (1999a) *Reviewing Performance and Pay of Heads and Deputy Heads: Guidance for governors*, London, DfEE.

Department for Education and Employment (1999b) *Performance Management Framework for Teachers: Consultation Document*, London, DfEE.

Teacher Training Agency (1997) *Effective Training Through Partnership: Working papers on secondary partnership*, London, TTA.

Teacher Training Agency (1998a) *National Standards for Qualified Teacher Status, Subject Leaders, Special Educational Needs Co-ordinators and Head Teachers*, London, TTA.

Teacher Training Agency (1998b) *Initial Teacher Training Curriculum: The use of information and communications technology in subject teaching*, London, TTA.

Further reading

Bleach, K. (2000) *The Induction and Mentoring of Newly Qualified Teachers*, London, David Fulton.

Addresses

The College of Teachers, The Old School, Coppice Row, Theydon Bois, tel: 01992 812 727, fax: 01992 814 690.

Teachers Appraisal and Training Scheme, Department for Education and Employment, Sanctuary Buildings, Great Smith Street, London SW1P 3BT, tel: 020 7925 5162, fax: 020 7925 6073.

Teacher Supply, Training and Qualifications Division, Sanctuary Buildings, Great Smith Street, London SW1P 3BT, tel: 020 7925 6014, fax: 020 7925 6073.

Teacher Training Agency, Portland House, Stag Place, London SE1E 5TT, tel: 020 7925 3700, fax: 020 7925 3792, e-mail: tta@gtnet.gov.uk

The Teacher Unit, Department for Education and Employment, Sanctuary Buildings, Great Smith Street, Westminster, London SW1P 3BT, tel: 020 7925 5000, fax: 020 7925 6000.

Pupil differences
Gender and ethnicity

A report on the attainment of pupils from ethnic minority groups (Her Majesty's Inspectors, 1999) looked at the way schools improve the attainment of pupils from Bangladeshi, Black Caribbean, Pakistani and Gypsy Traveller backgrounds. Visits by Her Majesty's Inspectors found that:

- the attainment of Bangladeshi and Pakistani pupils is 'lower than it should be' in the primary phase but improves once pupils are proficient in English;
- the performance of Black Caribbean pupils declines in secondary school; and
- the attainment of Gypsy Traveller children in secondary school is a cause of 'serious concern'.

Schools tend not to know how ethnic minority pupils are doing in important areas such as assessments and tests, attendance and behaviour. When information is available, it tends not to be used to plan future programmes. While school policy statements may be sound, they are not translated into effective practice. A school-wide approach is needed.

In the schools with the best practice, test results and other information was analysed and informed subsequent teaching strategies. The use of grant funded staff was not always sufficiently well thought out. Mentoring schemes worked well and study support and extracurricular activity helped pupils from ethnic minorities make progress. Only a minority of local education authorities (LEAs) had a clear strategy for improving the attainment of pupils from ethnic minority groups and LEAs do not carry out proper monitoring (Her Majesty's Inspectors, 1999).

The confusion of aspects of the education of pupils for whom English is an additional language with special educational needs is one area where greater clarity is needed at school level. At the national level there has been some lack of understanding about the population of pupils for whom English is an additional language. Is was originally assumed that the contribution of such children to overall school results would be such that in benchmarking, schools would need to allow for the effect of such pupils lowering the scores of the school overall. The tables guiding schools in benchmarking included a 'weighting' for such pupils. It emerged that the effect was not as strong as had been thought because of an admixture within the population of pupils for whom English is an additional language of pupils who were fluent in English and their first language.

Jane Addams, the social worker, defined civilisation as 'a method of living, an attitude of equal respect for all men.' Within this context, an issue which is not always sufficiently considered is the possible negative impact on other children's academic progress of the presence of many pupils for whom English is an additional language. In a forthright chapter, this issue is considered by John Rae in his *Letters to Parents* (Rae, 1998). Addressing the question of, 'might the presence of foreign pupils in the school hold back our child's education?' Rae takes the view that it might in an urban day school if there are a large number of pupils for whom English is a foreign or second language. Also acknowledged is the potential benefit of an international dimension to the school. The use of the International Baccalaureate may be an indication of a commitment to an international view.

With pupils for whom English is a second language, this does not of course mean that the pupil will be struggling with English. The pupil may speak several languages including English fluently. Where it does mean that a pupil has little command of the English language however, the school will need sufficient resources both in terms of physical resources and specialist staff support to ensure that these pupils make the progress expected. At the same time the school needs to ensure that pupils who have a good command of English are not held back or deprived of resources which they would otherwise have.

Further guidance is offered in the document *Removing the Barriers* (Department for Education and Employment, 2000). Four areas are seen as central:

- high expectations
- culture and ethos
- parental involvement
- ethnic monitoring.

High expectations may be supported by mentoring programmes and pupils being potential role models, and by structured learning and support programmes including an inclusive curriculum which considers and respects the cultural background of all pupils. In successful schools, the culture and ethos is characterised by such features as conscious efforts being made to redress the effects of stereotyping and prejudice, and procedures being established to deal with race relations in the school. Parental involvement is encouraged and made easier in successful schools through such methods as designating members of staff with a direct telephone link to parents, home visits, open-door sessions and language assistance. Ethnic monitoring involves analytical systems to monitor and assess pupils' academic progress and systems to monitor the effects of behaviour problems, truancy and exclusions.

Purported differences between boys and girls have been the source of much humour. Journalist Cyril Connolly considered that unlike girls, 'Boys do not grow up gradually. They move forward in spurts like the hands of clocks in railway stations.' Alexander Dumas, *fils*, said, 'It is only rarely that one can see in a little boy the promise of a man, but one can almost always see in a little girl the threat of a woman.'

In education, the debate about gender has moved on from simple observations about male and female roles in secondary school to a more complex consideration of differences that appear to involve the influence also of ethnicity and social status. Performance scores on national tests up to the age of 16 provide evidence of gender differences in achievement but also ethnicity, social class and religion combine with gender to influence performance. More boys than girls are identified as having special educational needs, have poor attendance and are excluded. Also boys grade their teachers lower than do girls and more boys than girls state that they do not enjoy school. At a national level, the difference in literacy attainment scores widens as children grow older. After the age of 16, boys tend to choose science and mathematics while girls choose arts and humanities.

The curriculum as the vehicle for teaching and learning has been studied from the gender perspective. For example, Davies (1998), considering the underperformance of boys, suggests that the linguistic behaviour of girls is more collaborative and less competitive than the behaviour of most boys, making it more valued in terms of National Curriculum assessments. Skelton (1998) intimates that physical education is governed by a set of 'macho' values, which pushes out girls and non-macho boys, and puts forward an argument for more inclusive physical education.

One implication of such studies is to consider whether the curriculum is sufficiently flexible to allow for and respond to the subtle ways in which teaching and learning interacts. It may be argued that the National Curriculum restricts opportunities to find flexible solutions to underachievement, which appears to be influenced by gender. However, the more the curriculum becomes open to change in content and method by teachers and students, the less able will anyone be to recognise any underachievement in the first place. The educational world could lapse into a caricature of the worst of 1960s self-indulgence in education where meeting supposed needs of pupils was traded for standards of attainment.

A more promising approach is to recognise the strengths of a National Curriculum and the proselytising of best practice, while at the same time remaining vigilant to ensure that the methods used in teaching and learning provide an education that benefits as many pupils as is possible.

In their equal opportunities policy, schools will already probably monitor the respective attainments of boys and girls in different areas of the curriculum and consider any trends and the action that might follow from this analysis. A more sophisticated approach to analysing the data than is sometimes taken may indicate the interrelation of social class, social status and race with apparent influences of gender. In developing the policy, schools are advised to ensure that parents, governors and all staff consider gender and related issues. When reviewing other policies the school will want to ensure that these reflect the school's commitment to equal opportunities.

Underachievement can be helped by classroom approaches. These include mixing underachievers and overachievers and conveying clear learning objectives for each lesson (perhaps by writing it where it is clearly visible for the whole lesson). Also, teachers could maintain a range of teaching styles, particularly group work, practical work, role play, discussion and active participation. Tasks could be organised one step at a time and information provided in manageable portions. Homework tasks can extend and enrich classroom work. They should be concise and short, and be assessed and returned speedily. When any work including homework is marked, it is particularly helpful to the pupil to give advice and comments on the work that conveys how the pupil can rectify a mistake or can improve.

Schools are advised to consider:

- monitoring the progress of all pupils including those for whom English is an additional language;
- ensuring that the school enjoys the advantages of a multicultural community, while making sure that pupils are not held back by the presence of pupils whose command of English is poor; and
- recognising in their analyses the likely interaction of the apparent effects of gender and other factors such as ethnicity, social class and religion.

References

Clarke, A. and Millard, E. (1998) *Gender in the Secondary Curriculum: Balancing the books*, London, Routledge.

Davies, J. (1998) 'Taking risks or playing safe' in Clarke, A. and Millard, E. (1998) *Gender in the Secondary Curriculum: Balancing the books*, London, Routledge.

Department for Education and Employment (2000) *Removing the Barriers: Raising achievement levels for minority ethnic pupils – key points for schools*, London, DfEE.

Her Majesty's Inspectors (1999) *Raising the Attainment of Ethnic Minority Pupils: School and LEA responses, HMI 170*, London, Office for Standards in Education.

Rae, J. (1998) *Letters to Parents*, London, HarperCollins.

Skelton, A. (1998) 'Eclipsed by Eton Fields' in Clarke, A. and Millard, E. (1998) *Gender in the Secondary Curriculum: Balancing the books*, London, Routledge.

Further reading

Schools Curriculum and Assessment Authority (1996) *Teaching English as an Additional Language: A framework for policy*, London, SCAA.

Address

National Association for Language Development in the Curriculum (NALDIC), S-W Herts LCSC, Hollywell JMI School Site, Tolpits Lane, Watford, Herts. WD1 8NT, tel: 01923 231 855, fax: 01923 225 130.

Quality approaches and project management

When assessing quality, one can be devious and indirect, as when W. S. Gilbert, the dramatist, said to an actor who had delivered a mediocre performance, 'My dear chap! Good isn't the word!' However, the more helpful assessments of quality are more direct and understandable.

The United States statistician W. Edwards Deming was responsible, along with Joseph Juran, for emphasising the importance of quality in post-war Japanese industry. According to Deming, all processes are vulnerable to loss of quality through variation. It follows from this, that if the levels of variation can be managed, then they can be decreased and quality can be raised. The key is the statistical control of quality. Among Deming's fourteen points for management are the following.

- Create constancy of purpose for continual improvement of products and service.
- Adopt and institute leadership aimed at helping people do a better job.
- Cease dependence on mass inspection: build quality into the product in the first place.
- End lowest tender contracts: instead require meaningful measures of quality along with price.
- Define top management's permanent commitment to ever-improving quality and productivity, and their obligation to implement all these principles.

The general point about decreasing levels of variation can be understood in school terms as using the school performance data as an indicator of the organisation's health and acting upon anything which shows variation from 'healthy' signs. Thus, if there is variation in attendance, action is taken in a timely and effective way. If interim tests indicate a lowering of predicted standards of pupil attainment, then steps are taken to rectify the situation in good time. Related to this, it is sometimes found in schools with serious weaknesses or under special measures that National

Curriculum test results and public examination grades are so variable from year to year as to be very difficult to predict.

How does a secondary school create constancy of purpose for continual improvement of products and service? Service can be understood in the school context as provision and product can be interpreted as outcomes, such as standards of pupil attainment or attendance figures.

Continual improvement in provision is a state of mind as well as a process. Each subject department can review its practices and procedures to see if there are better ways of doing things. Are there better resources? Is there a more effective way of deploying staff to achieve better results? Can the recruitment of staff be improved to attract better quality people? What strength in the quality of teaching can be consolidated and how can weaknesses be best remedied? These and many other features can form the basis of a continuing cycle of improvement. Improvements in outcomes are encouraged through such means as target setting and through improvements in provision.

Adopting and instituting leadership to help people do a better job keeps the focus on the facilitating aspect of leadership. Helping teachers teach better may involve monitoring quality of teaching and ensuring support and training to improve it. Performance management feeds into this. Implied in this is that all staff are clear about their roles and responsibilities.

The approach of ceasing dependence on mass inspection and building quality into the product in the first place is most obviously related to factory production. But it can be translated into the school setting. Instead of picking mistakes and poor standards up by monitoring and inspection, greater care can be taken with staff selection, good induction and training and setting high standards as the norm, so that inspection becomes mainly a confirmation of high quality rather than a fire-fighting exercise.

Requiring meaningful measures of quality along with price can translate into strategies of staff recruitment and performance management particularly when it is related to pay. The quality of performance can be expressed in recruitment literature, job descriptions and through the ethos of excellence among staff. The cost of achieving this in monetary terms will relate to the costs of recruitment, training and support. Relating quality to price is at the heart of initiatives to relate teachers' pay to performance.

How does one define top management's permanent commitment to ever-improving quality and productivity? This could relate to the roles of senior managers, their approach to monitoring and their general high expectations.

The approach to school self-evaluation is an aspect of improving quality. One way of synthesising the various models is to regard the Office for Standards in Education (OfSTED) inspection system as the underpinning model (Office for Standards in Education, 1999). This has the advantage of relating to more formal OfSTED inspections and prepares schools for this process. Other approaches, which can be used to complement the OfSTED model, are the Strathclyde model, the Basic Skills Quality Mark and the Investors in People initiative.

The Strathclyde model, developed by John Macbeath and his colleagues at Strathclyde University, involves the school reflecting on their values and principles and drafting criteria against which their work can be assessed. This developmental approach values qualitative measures as well as quantitative ones and involves everyone in the school community including pupils and parents.

The Basic Skills Quality Mark offers schools a structure for self-evaluation to help improve basic skills of pupils. The Quality Mark can also contribute to general school effectiveness. Ten elements are used for evaluation and all must be met before the Quality Mark is awarded.

The Investors in People (IIP) initiative was originally developed in industry and commerce and the public sector in the 1980s. It concentrates on the development of staff as a precurser to raising the achievement of pupils. Governors and senior staff must be committed to developing all staff.

Beacon schools are one way of trying to raise quality. Initially identified as centres of excellence, these schools are then funded so that their skills can be shared. They are eligible for grants for sharing their expertise among other schools.

Quality approaches like many other areas of the school can benefit from a project management approach. Three principles of project management are to:

• identify objectives and make sure that everyone is working to them and achieving them;
• establish flexible, responsive and forward-looking control; and
• ensure good-quality decision making.

The three traditional components of project management, namely time, cost and quality can be further elaborated. Time is closely related to cost in the sense that spending more money can buy time and spending more time can save money. Cost includes not just direct financial estimates but also other resources. Quality may be expressed in terms of measurable targets.

An example of work in a secondary school that could lend itself to a project management approach could be improving the grades of pupils taking General Certificate of Secondary Education (GCSE) examinations. The school would have to be specific about its targets, expressing them in measurable terms. The date at which the progress would be measured from, or the baseline, would be decided. The date at which the agreed target would be measured would also be specified. So the aims of the project might be expressed as increasing the percentage of students passing GCSE grade x and above in English from y per cent in the present year to z per cent two years later. This would in one sense also be the measure of quality. The time specified for the project is two years and the budget would be allocated according to the phases of the project which would be determined.

The objectives are clear, being to achieve the specified increase in GCSE English. The control would be exerted as the project developed to ensure that the project was on track. This would imply some continuing monitoring of the progress of pupils in English to ensure that they were progressing at the rate necessary to achieve the targets.

This leads to the steps that are necessary in the project. These would include identifying factors likely to improve progress. These might be good-quality stimulating physical resources, including books, compact discs, videos, audio-tapes and other resources, good teaching, strong systems to support teaching and other factors. This would imply a cost of buying or loaning physical resources and perhaps monitoring of the quality of teaching and any necessary training to ensure that it is good or better. Parallel with this, the school would need to identify factors that would inhibit progress and seek to remove or diminish them. In some instances, these factors would be the mirror image of the factors that encourage progress. An inhibiting factor would be poor pace in teaching, for example. In other cases, the negative factors could be identified and tackled. They might include a family home which is not conducive to home study. The school might consider what might be done to mitigate the effects of this, for example homework clubs.

The school will have now identified a range of factors, both those positive in their effect and those intended to mitigate potentially counterproductive influences. It will then work out a time plan in which the necessary actions will be put into place, for example, when the homework clubs will start and how they will operate.

The linking of approaches that focus on quality and methods that deliver results such as project management form a powerful combination.

The school is advised to consider:

- ensuring that its approaches are informed by quality management;
- using performance data to spot early signs of 'variation' or lowering standards;
- using the OfSTED model of school self-improvement as an underpinning structure supplemented by other models according to requirements; and
- clearly identifying those aspects of the school's work which will lend themselves to a project management approach.

Reference

Office for Standards in Education (1999) *Handbook for Inspecting Secondary Schools with Guidance on Self-Evaluation*, London, The Stationery Office.

Addresses

Association of Project Managers, Westbourne Street, High Wycombe, Buckinghamshire HP11 2PZ, tel: 01494 440 090, fax: 01494 528 937, e-mail: secretariat@apm-uk.demon.co.uk

The Basic Skills Agency, Commonwealth House, 1–19 New Oxford Street, London WC1A 1NU, tel: 020 7405 4017, fax: 020 7404 5038, e-mail: enquiries@basic-skills.co.uk   web-site: www.basic-skills.co.uk

Investors in People (IIP), 7 Chandos Street, London W1, tel: 020 7467 1900, fax: 020 7636 2386, e-mail: info@iipuk.co.uk

Office for Standards in Education (OfSTED), Alexander House, 29–33 Kingsway, London, tel: 020 7421 6800, fax: 020 7421 6707, e-mail: alexandrahouse@ofsted.gov.uk

Resources and their best use

Resources are always important. A cabman complained to Lord Rothschild that the tip he had just handed over was only half of the gratuity that Rothschild's son had given only a few days earlier. Lord Rothschild bristled. 'I know,' he said. 'My son has a millionaire for a father and I haven't.'

Time is a resource and any approaches that seek to optimise its full use are worth considering. In this light the debates about the five-term year and alternative calendars and the fuller use of staff time in summer schools and other provisions are an important and developing trend. The fuller use of the school premises adds to resources. This includes letting to community groups and others to benefit those groups and raise funds for the school, and using the premises for the school's own pupils through lunchtime clubs, after-school activities and summer schools. Although a wider definition of resources includes time and human resources, most of the present section focuses on learning resources, excluding premises.

Learning resources range from computers and software to gymnastics equipment and mathematics texts. The effectiveness of a learning resource can be assessed in various ways but a key factor must be the impact it has on raising standards of pupil attainment. The initial cost of a purchased resource can be weighed against the alternative costs such as renting or sharing with another school. Acquisition of the resource can be viewed in the light of the amount of use the resource is given. The longevity of the resource is another factor, as is the cost of its replacement.

Improvements in the effectiveness of the resources can similarly be achieved in various ways. The use of a resource can be increased by raising the staff's awareness of the existence of the resource, its potential usefulness, or improving its availability. The cost of a resource can be reduced through buying in bulk or through sharing the cost with another school and possibly through agreeing its shared use. The longevity of a resource may be extended by treating it (for example by laminating books) or by having clear rules for its use (such as using an expensive piece of equipment only with supervision).

For instance, consider the effectiveness of a scheme of published material in mathematics. The initial cost of the scheme would be considered as well as the cost of replacing books and related materials over a period of, say, five years. The use of the scheme could be increased by ensuring that it was kept centrally so that it could be used by the maximum number of classes taking into account the timetables and the times when the scheme would be used. In-service training could inform staff of the potential benefits of the scheme to ensure its best use. Encouraging staff and pupils to take care of it could extend the longevity of the scheme. Monitoring of the effect on standards could help any judgement about the longer-term usefulness of the scheme, of course supplemented with other materials.

An educational resource that is not always fully used is the classroom display. This may include the work of pupils that is displayed to demonstrate the value that is placed on good-quality work and to improve the classroom learning environment. However, once displays have been put up, are they used sufficiently as a learning aid? Is a history display subsequently used by pupils, directed by the teacher if necessary, to check facts or to aid interpretation? Perhaps the literature display could help pupils by providing models of good essay structure.

Businesses can help in ensuring that a school has good-quality resources. Sydney Smith the British clergyman said, 'You never expected justice from a company did you? They have neither a soul to lose nor a body to kick.' By contrast Woodrow Wilson took the view that, 'Business underlies everything in our national life, including our spiritual life. Witness the fact that in the Lord's prayer the first petition is for daily bread. No one can worship God or love his neighbour on an empty stomach.' Schools need to take a pragmatic view of particular deals which are offered to them or which they seek.

Sponsored teaching materials are an increasingly useful source of resources if the school develops a suitable process of selecting what materials would be fitting. One form of selection is to consider materials that are written by teachers employed by the company and which are endorsed by subject associations. The key test is the educational value of the resources and if a school can say that if the resources were on sale by a commercial company, they would still be interested in purchasing them, then this is a good yardstick.

The National Consumer Council (1996) has developed voluntary guidelines concerning sponsorship, advertising and marketing products. These offer advice, which is widely agreed to be sensible, to businesses and others regarding publishing educational resources. The aim is to help ensure that all materials and activities achieve high standards of quality, balance and integrity. The marketing message needs to be balanced by genuine educational content and benefit. The guidelines cover:

- educational value and curriculum relevancy;
- balance and objectivity;
- consultation and testing;
- sales and promotional messages;
- sponsored gifts, awards, voucher schemes and other promotional/ marketing activities;
- unsolicited marketing activity;
- avoiding stereotypes; and
- description and labelling.

Education–Business Partnerships are also useful organisations to contact, as are Science and Technology Regional Organisations (SATROs). National Training Organisations (NTOs) such as the Steel NTO can provide information on current industry-related curriculum materials.

As a method of government control, along with local education action plans and the possibility of privatisation, the Standards Fund offers incentives for following government initiatives. Government Circulars invite local education authorities in England to apply for grant support on their expenditure in each financial year through the Standards Fund.

There are several levels of grant support and local education authorities (LEAs) are expected often to contribute a percentage, although grants sometimes cover the whole amount. LEAs are expected to make sure that the maximum amount of Standards Fund grant is devolved to schools. Decisions regarding the Standards Fund should be needs led within the requirements of each grant.

There are three kinds of grant: competitive, formula-based and pre-selected. With competitive grants, LEAs bid for a share of funds and are informed later whether they have been successful. For formula-based grants, LEAs receive a notional allocation related to such factors as the number of schools. In the case of pre-selected grants, some LEAs, schools or schemes are chosen to receive grants, while others are not.

Recent grants have covered areas including the following:

- access fund for post-16 pupils in schools; administrative support for small schools; advanced skills teachers;
- early retirement scheme for headteachers; early years training and development; education and health partnerships; ethnic minority and traveller achievement grant; excellence in cities;
- improving adult/pupil ratios in reception classes;
- local authority support for life-long learning;
- National Curriculum; national grid for learning; national literacy and numeracy strategies;
- parent governors; performance management and threshold assessment training; pilot education maintenance allowance; playing for success; protecting and expanding local authority music services;

- qualifications;
- school improvement; school leadership; school security; small school support; social inclusion; special educational needs; specialist schools and beacon schools; study support;
- teacher incentives; teaching assistants; training schools;
- working environment.

It is helpful if schools are aware of the allocation of these grants and the implications for their income so that this informs budget projections. LEAs should inform schools of devolved Standards Funds before the start of the financial year, so that schools can plan for the expenditure for the forthcoming year.

The school is advised to consider:

- auditing the initial and maintenance cost of resources;
- monitoring the use of the resource;
- having clear routines for the care of resources;
- assessing the effect of the resource on raising standards;
- being fully aware of the categories of Standards Fund bids and the expected grants so that it can plan its budget; and
- ensuring that the LEA is gaining access to the funding appropriate to the needs of local schools.

Reference

National Consumer Council (1996) *Sponsorship in Schools: Good practice guidelines*, London, NCC.

Further reading

British Educational Suppliers Association (annually) *The Complete Guide to British Educational Supply*, London, BESA.
University of Warwick (1999) *Directory of Teaching Materials* from Business University of Warwick Centre for Education and Industry.

Addresses

British Educational Suppliers Association (BESA) 20 Beaufort Court, Admirals Way, London E14 9XL, tel: 020 7537 4997, fax: 020 7537 4846, web-site: www.besanet.org.uk
Local Education Authority Finance, Department for Education and Employment, Sanctuary Buildings, Great Smith Street, London SW1P 3BT, tel: 020 7925 6086, fax: 020 7925 6988.
National Consumer Council, 20 Grosvenor Gardens, London SW1H 0DH, tel: 020 7730 3469, fax: 020 7730 0191, e-mail: info@ncc.org.uk

School Business Initiatives Unit, Department for Education and Employment, Sanctuary Buildings, Great Smith Street, Westminster, London SW1P 3BT, tel: 020 7925 5000, fax: 020 7925 6000.

School improvement plans

Optimising their effect

Dr Samuel Johnson said that most schemes of political improvement are 'very laughable things'. Schemes for school improvement, however, are often useful if they are kept as simple as possible and if they do not bury themselves in detail.

School improvement has been described (Office for Standards in Education, 1994) as the ways in which schools: raise standards, enhance quality, increase efficiency, and achieve greater success in promoting pupils' spiritual, moral, social and cultural development (ethos of the school). These are the themes of the Framework for the Inspection of Schools (Office for Standards in Education, 1999).

School effectiveness concerns how a school is currently performing and is mainly based on outcomes. 'School effectiveness' suggests targets and 'improvement' implies strategies for reaching those targets. 'Improvement' is the potential for raising achievement over a particular period and involves processes. The two notions are interrelated. Also interrelated are whole school improvement, departmental improvement and individual class improvement. A struggling school may not be able to improve itself but may need outside help to start the process.

School improvement plans are the systematic drawing together of areas otherwise covered in the school development plan, the action plan following an inspection by the Office for Standards in Education (OfSTED), or in any local education education authority (LEA) or school evaluation and monitoring process or documentation.

The four OfSTED areas of raising standards, enhancing quality, increasing efficiency, and improving the school ethos have the advantage of being central to education. At the same time these aspects of improvement are part of the OfSTED Framework which guides OfSTED inspectors and informs their judgements. This in turn informs the action plan that schools develop after an OfSTED inspection, which integrates with school planning for improvement. Therefore, if schools were to adopt the definition, it would inform their self-evaluation and would also help ensure that the improvements brought about by an OfSTED inspection fitted the same understanding of improvement.

Another point is whether it is a reasonable expectation for a school to continuously improve. In the OfSTED publication *Improving Schools*, this expectation is clear. The publication states that schools have much in common regarding the provision they make and the framework in which they operate. It goes on to say that not only are the ways in which they deliver that provision 'infinitely varied' but that they are also 'infinitely improvable'.

If targets are based on standardised test results over a period of time, then, depending on the quality and suitability of the test, these could have credibility. Where targets are based on national test and task results, improvements may be less meaningful depending on the degree to which tests change from year to year. A school could, for example, use standardised test results and then look for value-added indicators.

How daunting is this for a school? A headteacher, governors and others may agree on challenging targets, for example in increasing the percentage of pupils reaching agreed levels in National tests in reading. Through hard work, the target is achieved and the following year an even more challenging target is agreed.

At some point, would the school not find that despite enormous effort, little or no increase occurs in the pupils reaching the agreed levels in reading? Such a position and the perceived increased possibility of failure may discourage those setting the targets from being as ambitious as they would otherwise be.

However, it could be accepted that a good position has been reached with regard to a particular target, such as the one in our example. The task for the following year would be to ensure that that position was maintained at least and that attention be turned to another target. This may well of course be another English target of which there could be many over the years, each genuinely contributing to raising standards in the subject. The point is that there is always another aspect of a subject, or the curriculum, or the school as a whole that can be improved.

It could be argued that the efforts of a school in one area of the curriculum or of an aspect of school life would take effort away from another area or aspect of school life. If this was a previous target area, this might lead to a decline in that area. However, counterbalancing this is the cumulative effect that success and improvement in one area has on improvement in another. Some areas directly interrelate, such as spiritual, moral, social and cultural provision, or mathematical aspects of geography and science, to take only two examples. Other cumulatively beneficial effects are more general, such as the improvement in staff, pupil and parent morale created by improvements in one area, which can carry over to others, including those that were the subject of previous targets.

Senior managers and governors should have clear models of managing school improvement and should be skilful in implementing them. Such models, based on practice in industry, have been put forward. Industrial and business planners are concerned with audit, direction, strategies and evaluation. Drawing on these, four fundamental questions can be asked:

- Where is the school at present?
- What changes are necessary?
- How shall change be managed?
- How shall we know whether the management of change has succeeded?

The question 'Where is the school at present?' is addressed by an audit and contributing to this is the information that will have been shared with the school when it received its OfSTED inspection. Audits by local education authority inspectors and others and audits conducted by the school itself will also contribute.

Regarding the question 'What changes are necessary?', a very challenging part of the process is deciding these and ensuring that they are specific, realistic and achievable, yet challenging. It is important, where appropriate, to consider a range of ways in which goals can be reached and assessing the alternatives before deciding on the best approach.

Turning to the question 'How shall change be managed?', the way in which the changes are made and their systematic management is often essential to the success or failure of the venture.

An evaluation of the whole process is implied in the question 'How shall we know whether the management of change has succeeded?' The importance of this lies in the learning it generates so that lessons can be learned from what went right and what went wrong in the process. Although this consumes time, it can also save time with regard to later changes as more refined and robust approaches are developed.

Similar points are built into a Department for Education and Employment (DfEE) model of a cycle of school self-improvement. The key questions are as follows:

- 'How well are we doing?' (e.g. information from OfSTED and the Qualifications and Curriculum Authority)
- 'How well do we compare with similar schools?' (see in the present volume 'Benchmarking: Comparing like with like?')
- 'What more could we aim to achieve this year?' (see in the present volume 'Target setting: Behind the jargon')
- 'What must we do to make it happen?' (development planning)

This leads to taking action and reviewing progress. These issues are central to an effective school development plan. An example of a good plan (OfSTED, 1994) includes the points explicitly and involves:

1. current expectations, considering national policies and the school's aims and objectives (this informs the audit);
2. current practice and provision and their effectiveness (part of the audit, addressing the question 'Where are we now?');
3. realistic but challenging targets (partly addressing the question, 'Where do we want to go?');
4. other aspects of the school development plan of course include allocating tasks, setting a time scale, agreeing on the people involved, dealing with the training and staff development implications and agreeing the resources needed including money (these contribute to the strategies for reaching the targets and address the question, 'How do we get there?');
5. success criteria (part of the question, 'How do we know when we have got there?'); and
6. monitoring and progress check (part of the evaluation of the whole, that is school self-evaluation).

As well as the broad view of improving achievement, the more detailed related issues will need consideration. What evidence is there of underachievement and is this with all pupils or most of them? Are some pupils not progressing as well as they could be because they appear to be resting on their laurels? Is the school performing well with both high and low achievers? Is the school performing well with both boys and girls? Is there differential departmental subject effectiveness?

We have considered school improvement mainly in relation to the raising of academic standards. But other aspects of school life are important. For example, improving efficiency could encompass reductions in the financial deficit in a school's budget. Improving ethos could include observable improvements in pupil behaviour.

The National Foundation of Educational Research (NFER) School Improvement Research Centre is carrying out several projects. These include an action research project sponsored by the DfEE on raising standards through self-evaluation. NFER have also completed a review of strategies of school self-evaluation.

Ways in which school improvement is encouraged include school development planning, sharing aspirations and criteria for success, quality control and hard work. Increasingly, lesson observations are central to show that there is improvement in the teaching in classrooms.

The document *Improving Schools* (Office for Standards in Education, 1994) identifies elements of improvements in certain case-study schools that it is thought other schools could replicate. These are:

- realism about what the school is and is not achieving;
- ambition for tangible, specific improvements;

- systems for planning and target setting;
- rigour in sticking to agreed deadlines, meetings, tasks to be completed;
- partnership between staff, governors and parents;
- open sharing of aspirations and criteria for success by senior managers, teachers, governors, parents and pupils;
- self-criticism in continuing analysis and identification of areas needing improvement within a culture of self-evaluation;
- praise and acknowledgement for every sign of improvement;
- willingness to continue searching for excellence and to keep on believing that the school, its pupils and teachers are capable of achieving it.

This approach is reflected in the OfSTED approach to school self-evaluation. This concerns establishing the point which the school has reached, where one begins, evaluating standards and teaching, giving feedback after lesson observations and ongoing support, performance management and leading improvement and using inspection to complement the self-evaluation process. A cultural change began in the 1990s and continued into the new century as teachers and headteachers became more confident in handling data, evaluating teaching and learning processes and converting these evaluations into meaningful action.

References

Office for Standards in Education (1999) *Handbook for Inspecting Secondary Schools with Guidance on Self-Evaluation*, London, The Stationery Office.

Office for Standards in Education (1994) *Improving Schools*, London, Her Majesty's Stationery Office.

Further reading

Department for Education and Employment (1997) *Excellence in Schools (White Paper) Cm. 3681*, London, The Stationery Office.

Department for Education and Employment and Office for Standards in Education (1997) *From Targets to Action: Guidance to support effective target setting in schools (Improving Schools Series)* London, DfEE, Standards and Effectiveness Unit.

Office for Standards in Education (1998) *School Evaluation Matters*, London, OfSTED.

Saunders, L. and Stradling, R. with Gallagher, S. (1996) *Raising Attainment in Secondary Schools: A handbook for school self evaluation,* Slough, National Foundation for Educational Research.

Address

School Improvement Research Centre, National Foundation of Educational
  Research, The Mere, Upton Park, Slough, Berkshire SL1 2DQ, tel: 01753 574 123,
  fax: 01753 691 632, e-mail: eval&pol@nfer.ac.uk   web-site: www.nfer.ac.uk

Special educational needs
Some recent trends

In *Macbeth*, Shakespeare writes, 'Confusion now hath made his master-piece'. In the sphere of special education, it would be an exaggeration to describe the 1997 Green Paper similarly but there were aspects requiring further clarity. The Green Paper *Excellence for All Children: Meeting special educational needs* (Department for Education, 1997a) concerned raising standards, shifting resources to practical support and increasing inclusion. Building on an earlier consultation paper (Kilfoyle, 1997) and views signalled by the White Paper *Excellence in Schools* (Department for Education and Employment, 1997b), the Green Paper set out the future blueprint for special education.

It endorses early intervention but does not acknowledge that early intervention schemes tend to require large sums of money spent over a considerable period of time to have a lasting impact. American projects such as Headstart and research into early deprivation indicate that successful early intervention requires substantial resources and continued positive discrimination.

The Green Paper interprets early intervention as better identification and improved multi-agency co-operation. Resources might be 'shifted' but new money is unlikely to be forthcoming. Also, early intervention seems to be associated with young people, whereas it is equally important for children whose difficulties arise or become unmanageable later.

Target setting in 'mainstream' schools may encourage teachers to concentrate time and other resources on pupils at the cusp of level achieving five good General Certificate of Secondary Education (GCSE) examinations. This is because schools are striving to reach levels which will show up favourably in league tables. Depending on local circumstances some schools may not be expected to reach the national targets while others will exceed them. The effect of these national targets could be to squeeze provision for pupils with special educational needs (SENs). At the same time schools are encouraged to include more pupils with SENs and the two approaches appear incompatible.

Schools need to set targets against a stable background. If inclusion increases the number of children with SENs in ordinary schools, this is likely to have implications for the targets set by the school. Yet there is no machinery for adjusting achievement targets to reflect the inclusion of pupils with SENs.

On entry, assessment extends to pupils who may have SENs and its use as a value-added measure is being developed. Where schools are concerned that the inclusion of pupils with SENs might adversely affect their overall achievement results, value-added measures seem to be put forward as a solution. But it remains to be seen whether these are as credible as more 'absolute' measures of achievement. Some parents select a school not according to value added but on the absolute results achieved as an indication of the level at which the school is working. Such parents would pick a school where pupils achieved well rather than one in which pupils had progressed well from a lower starting point but achieved at an inferior level in absolute terms. The exception to this is perhaps the choice of a school made by the parent of a child who has SENs, but such a choice could lead to an overconcentration of pupils with SENs in one ordinary school.

For benchmarking, schools will compare themselves with supposedly similar schools. Comparisons will take into account pupils' eligibility for free school meals but not SENs. If benchmarking does not reflect the relative inclusion by different schools of pupils with SENs, it is hard to see how schools otherwise similar but with different levels of inclusion could be fairly compared.

The Green Paper proposed to maintain a parent's present right to express a preference for a special school place for their child where they believe it necessary But in practice, a parent's preference may not be met. If parental preference is not accepted, there will have to be criteria for acceptance or rejection.

Parents will have a right to express a preference for a special school 'where they consider it appropriate to their child's needs'. There is a difference of course between expressing a preference for a school and getting a place in that school as all parents know, whether or not their child has special educational needs. But all those involved will need to avoid a bias towards the more articulate parent perhaps from a more privileged background being able to express their preference more effectively than other parents. Parent support groups might help ensure equity. It is said that children should be enrolled in ordinary schools unless there are 'compelling reasons' for doing otherwise. It is not apparent whether parental preference for a special school constitutes such a reason.

Where schools make contextual judgements about the children with SENs in the school these may relate to the level of skills of the teacher and other school factors, as much as the difficulties that the child experiences. This can lead to inequities in the number of children who are considered to have SENs in various schools that appear quite similar. Where schools receive higher levels of funding according to their number of children with SENs, there may be an incentive to identify children and a disincentive to move them off the register of SENs or to end the life of a statement. National criteria may address some of these inequities but at the expense of being sufficiently sensitive to some genuine school context issues.

Furthermore, research at the London School of Economics Centre for Educational Research by Anne West, Hazel Pennel, Tony Travers and Robert West indicates that the proportion of pupils with statements of special educational need is not related to other indicators of 'need' such as poverty (*Times Educational Supplement*, 1999). This, the researchers believe, may relate to the skills of middle-class parents using the system better to gain the extra cash associated with statements.

Presumably, if current practice gives excessive prominence to statements this indicates that government wishes to reduce the cost of the bureaucracy of statements. If so, local education authorities (LEAs) should also look carefully at the very high costs of maintaining children in schools outside the LEA area. Inclusion would then encompass the transfer of these 'out-of-borough' children to local day special schools for instance.

The provision of a special school seems to be understood as comprising the skills of staff which can be exercised in other settings or which can be conveyed to teachers in ordinary schools. But there are aspects of special schools integral to the whole school. An example of this is the boundaries both physical and psychological of a good special school (especially for children with emotional and behavioural difficulties). Other examples are the concentration of staff expertise built upon by regular contact with other highly skilled colleagues and the close monitoring of pupils made possible by the small class sizes in special schools. Further instances are the economical concentration of physical resources in a place where they will be fully used, and the location of specialist staff among a group of children who need their services.

Related to the notion of teacher skills, care needs to be taken over the type and extent of training to help equip a teacher in an ordinary school with the skills needed to teach pupils with perhaps different and more complex SENs than previously. A simple model of skills, knowledge and experience seems unsuitable for such a situation, but some kind of structure is necessary for training.

One approach would be to develop placements in special schools for teachers in ordinary schools so that they can develop practice with a mentor and the whole school support framework of a good special school. Different stages of teacher training and education might gradually introduce involvement with good special schools. These might begin with visits and team teaching in special schools in early initial teacher training. They could develop into teaching in a special school as part of the professional development of a well-established ordinary school teacher.

Meeting Special Educational Needs: A programme of action (1998) includes a timetable summarising action over the three years following its publication. The 'Programme' builds on the Green Paper *Excellence for All Children*. Support and advice given to parents would be improved to enable them to be more involved in the education of their child. Government would provide high-quality child care and early years education. Earlier identification of difficulties and early intervention as necessary would be encouraged. Every LEA would have a parent partnership scheme by 1999 allowing parents access to advice from an independent supporter. LEAs would have conciliation arrangements for settling disagreements. Stronger arrangements would be made to involve children in the SEN process.

Government intended to build on existing statutory provisions and best practice to improve the SEN framework and to better focus on meeting children's SENs. A simplified SEN Code of Practice would be introduced in 2000/2001 (in fact this was delayed) concentrating on preventative work, reducing bureaucracy and promoting effective school-based support and monitoring. Guidance would be published on the placement of children under the Code and the related provision. Criteria would be brought out for making statements of SEN. LEAs would have to publish more comprehensive information about their SEN policies. This would include information about what schools might normally provide from their own budgets and information about the SEN support that LEAs would provide. Performance would be monitored against key indicators. Government would seek to improve the effectiveness of the SEN Tribunal.

Government intended to promote further inclusion and develop the role of special schools. From 1999, LEAs would publish information about their policy on inclusion in their Education Development Plans. The statutory framework for inclusion (section 316 of the Education Act 1996) would be reviewed. Government would identify and disseminate good practice by special schools in developing practical links with mainstream schools. The contribution of special schools to an increasingly inclusive education system would be promoted. Steps would be taken to ensure that children with SENs are treated fairly in schools' admissions procedures. Financial support would be provided for projects aiming to improve provision and raise achievements for children with emotional and behavioural difficulties.

Greater emphasis would be given to SEN within teacher training and development. Good practice guidance would be published on the work of learning support assistants. In 1999, consultation would take place on a description of the future role of educational psychologists. Government would consider further the particular training and development needs of staff working with children with SENs in the light of consultation on the planned Green Paper on the future of the teaching profession.

Government intend to help improve the way that LEAs work together, and in partnership with other local agencies, to strengthen support for children with SENs. From April 2000, regional co-ordination of SEN provision would be extended across the country. New duties of partnership and new powers would be introduced to enable more flexible funding arrangements between the National Health Service and local authorities. Initiatives would be developed to improve the provision of speech and language therapy services. Information would be gathered about the experiences, once they have left school, of young people with SENs, to help schools and colleges prepare young people for adult life more effectively. These developments would be supported through more effective collaboration between government departments, particularly the DfEE and the Department of Health.

Many of these aspirations have since been implemented. For some of the developments, the same reservations exist as those outlined in connection with the SEN Green Paper. Time will tell what their effect will be but no one could accuse the government of standing still. If anything the concern is that the pace of change is so rapid that consultation seems superficial and the interactive effect of some of the changes cannot be known.

Schools are advised to consider:

• being aware of the implications of the Green Paper, the Programme for Action and subsequent developments; and
• giving particular thought to aspects where government policies appear to be pulling in different directions.

References

Department for Education (1997a) *Excellence for All Children: Meeting special educational needs*, London, DfEE.
Department for Education (1997b) *Excellence in Schools*, London, DfEE.
Department for Education (1998) *Meeting Special Educational Needs: A programme of action*
Kilfoyle, P. (1997) *Every Child is Special: Proposals to improve special needs education*, London, Labour Party.
Qualifications and Curriculum Authority (1997) *Baseline Assessment Scales for Children with Special Educational Needs: Teachers guide*, London, QCA.
Schools Curriculum and Assessment Authority (1997) *Baseline Assessment Scales*, London, SCAA.
Times Educational Supplement (1999) 'Ministers told cash pays off in results', Friday 11 June 1999, no. 4328, p. 1.

Further reading

Department for Education and Employment (1998) *Meeting Special Educational Needs: A programme of action*, London, DfEE.

Department for Education and Employment (2000) *SEN Code of Practice on the Assessment and Identification of Pupils with Special Educational Needs*, London, DFEE.

Addresses

National Association for Special Educational Needs (NASEN), NASEN House, 4–5 Amber Business Village, Amber Close, Amington, Tamworth, Staffordshire, B77 4RP, tel: 01827 311 500, fax: 01827 313 005, e-mail: nasen@bbcnc.org.uk

Special Educational Needs Policy Division, Department for Education and Employment, Sanctuary Buildings, Great Smith Street, Westminster, London WC1, tel: 020 7925 6434, fax: 020 7925 6986.

Standards and effectiveness

The terms standards and effectiveness express many issues related to school improvement. The Education Act 1996 includes measures to raise standards in schools. These include requiring schools to set targets for improving their performance, and giving Office for Standards in Education (OfSTED) powers to inspect the effectiveness of local education authorities (LEAs). Assessment measures are another way in which it is hoped to raise achievement. These somewhat external measures continue alongside measures which are more internal to the school such as school self-improvement initiatives. Effectiveness can mean a variety of things.

An important aspect of improving standards is that of ensuring that money is well spent and focusing it on raising standards. For anyone who underestimates the importance of managing budgets and the general importance of handling money effectively, the observations of United States of America statesman Woodrow Wilson are pertinent. 'Business underlies everything in our national life, including our spiritual life,' he proclaimed. 'Witness the fact that in the Lord's prayer the first petition is for our daily bread. No one can worship God or love his neighbour on an empty stomach.'

As part of the emphasis on value for money, it is increasingly important that schools are not only aware of the standards of pupil attainment, other standards in the school and the trends in these but also the relative cost of achieving them.

In some areas, such as special educational needs (SEN), schools are unclear about their income, how it is spent and what the results are. It is not difficult to find SEN co-ordinators who do not know how much money the school gets for their area, making any attempts to improve efficiency cosmetic.

In the OfSTED model (Office for Standards in Education, 1999) budgeting relates particularly to the efficiency of the school. Inspectors have to report on how well the school is led and managed. This includes the extent to which the school makes the best strategic use of resources, including specific grants and additional funding, 'linking decisions on spending to educational priorities'. Among the areas which inspectors explore in relation to this area is to judge how well educational priorities are supported through careful financial management and planning. Another aspect is judging whether effective use is made of new technologies, and whether specific grants are used effectively for their designated purpose.

The role of the governing body is to oversee financial management, ensuring that the school is able to account for expenditure, budgets for new expenditure and analyses the use of its resources regularly. Inspectors assess the impact of the decisions made by the school in the way that funding is used regarding its educational priorities and to cause improvement.

The Standards Fund is an important source of targeted funding. LEAs in England apply for this grant support on their expenditure in each financial year. The range of grants mirrors the government's priority of raising standards in schools as set out in the White Paper *Excellence in Schools* published on 7 July 1997. The main focus is on school self-improvement through targets agreed with the LEA and embodied in the school and LEA development plans.

Most of the Standards Fund is allocated to schools with LEAs supporting schools in raising standards. From 1998 LEA targets and priorities were reflected in Education Development Plans (EDPs). Activities funded through the Standards Fund should not replicate activities funded through LEA resources or other government grants like the Single Regeneration Budget.

The programme reflects the national priorities for teacher professional development as seen by the Teacher Training Agency. Schools and LEAs should follow certain principles to underpin professional development.

Development opportunities should be targeted through needs assessment and appraisal. Professional development activities should address needs through quality assurance of the provision. It should be ensured that professional development has the maximum impact on classroom practice through monitoring and evaluating development activities and setting improvement targets. The five non-contact days should be used as part of schools' planned programmes of professional development. School governors should be accountable for the professional development of staff and its impact on teaching and learning. Schools and LEAs are expected to ensure all this.

Grants attract a higher rate of support if government is particularly keen to encourage an approach. LEAs submit bids competitively. For most grants, allocations are formula based, for example according to the number of schools or pupils.

LEAs cannot delegate the Standards Fund supported expenditure to schools via the Aggregated Schools Budget. This is precluded by the

Education (Financial Delegation to Schools) (Mandatory Exemptions) Regulations 1995 (Statutory Instrument 1995/178). LEAs are asked to confirm that all expenditure supported by the devolved Standards Fund grants will be met from resources held centrally by the LEA within its General Schools Budget. This expenditure includes the LEA's own required contribution. The LEA cannot draw on schools' own delegated budget shares.

The individual entries indicate the expenditure eligible for support within the devolved grants, although schools are allowed to determine their own pattern of expenditure. Schools should keep clear records of expenditure available for audit.

LEAs should involve schools closely in developing and implementing school-related grants under the Standards Fund. Among the grants that have been involved in the Standards Fund are the following: assessment, drug prevention and schools, early years training and development, family literacy, and improving attendance and behaviour. The grants also cover: the induction of newly qualified teachers, national literacy project – key stage 3, premier league club study sports centres, qualifications, reduction of infant class sizes, and school effectiveness. Standards Funding includes grants for school leadership, service, school security, specialist schools, special educational needs, specialist teacher assistants, summer literacy schools, and work-related learning.

The role of independent schools is important. It is not difficult to find someone critical of the independent school system or of particular independent schools. Novelist Evelyn Waugh said, 'Anyone who has been to an English public school will always feel comparatively at home in prison.' However, the best independent schools can make a valuable contribution to raising standards for all.

The Labour government elected in the late 1990s began their tenure with a gesture – no more – apparently against the independent sector. The assisted places scheme, which has helped pupils who would not otherwise have been able to do so to attend independent schools, was abolished. The intention was to use this small sum towards paying for smaller classes in all state primary schools. Yet, in its approach, the government requested the support of independent schools in improving education for all.

A £1.6 million programme encouraged partnerships between independent and state schools. Altogether, 199 schools participated in the two-year programme announced by the schools minister Estelle Morris in May 1999. Approaches include some shared lessons, the sharing of expertise on special educational needs and the use of information and communications technology.

Links may be built upon common goals of striving for excellence even when the intake of the school makes this not excellence in absolute terms but in value-added terms. These may be schools for pupils with general or specific learning difficulties, where higher than usual progress is made.

The links if they can be successfully formed relate to the sharing of such things as common teaching, resources, best practice and the importance of academic qualifications between the best state schools and the best private-sector schools. John Rae, former headmaster of Westminster School, traces the change of emphasis in the independent sector to the 1990s (Rae, 1998). Before then the primary purpose of many independent schools was to instil the qualities of leadership, service and character. Character was encouraged by juniors learning to take orders from seniors in the school. As the juniors grew older, they would develop qualities of leadership as prefects and would serve the community. As A levels became the standard currency for university entrance, gaining these academic qualifications became increasingly important. Parents began to look to independent schools to offer this, particularly as they could see the best state grammar schools achieving better academic results than some fee-paying independent schools.

Some individual development indicated the possible direction of future developments. From September 2000, the Belvedere School, an independent day school for girls in Toxteth, Liverpool, admitted pupils aged 11 years on academic merit, disregarding the parent's ability to pay the school's fees. The cost is shared equally between two trusts.

While independent schools have employed for some time development directors under various titles. The main role of the development director is to seek additional funding and support from various quarters. For some independent schools, the loss of assisted places has placed extra demands on this role. In the state sector, Lancaster Royal Grammar School in 1996–7 became one of the first schools to employ a development director.

Among the factors encouraging such appointments are the financial responsibilities of many state schools. These include delegated funding giving greater financial control to schools, business links and sponsorship, marketing, tapping sources of income such as government money through bids, fund raising, business partnerships, income generation, marketing, public relations and alumni support. The benefits of having one specialist person to co-ordinate all this are becoming increasingly apparent.

Schools are advised to consider:

- having transparent budgets that reflect the costs incurred in raising standards;
- ensuring that spending decisions are informed by their effect on raising standards;
- recognising the importance of academic excellence in the best of state and independent schools; and

- having a clear identity for raising standards even though this might be from a lower starting point than many schools.

References

Department for Education and Employment (1997) *Circular 13/97: The Standards Fund 1998–99*, London, DfEE.
Office for Standards in Education (1999) *The OfSTED Handbook for the Inspection of Secondary Schools*, London, Her Majesty's Stationery Office.
Rae, J. (1998) *Letters to Parents*, London, HarperCollins.

Further reading

Institute of Development Professional in Education (1999) *Principles and Standards of Professional Practice*, Manchester, IDP.

Addresses

Independent Schools Information Service (ISIS), 35–37 Grosvenor Gardens, London, SW1W 0BS, tel: 020 7798 1500, fax: 020 7798 1501, e-mail: national @isis.org.uk
Institute of Development Professionals in Education, PO Box 102, Manchester M14 6XE, tel: 0161 434 1847, e-mail: info@idpe.org.uk web-site: www. idpe.org.uk
Local Education Authority Finance, Department for Education and Employment, Sanctuary Buildings, Great Smith Street, London SW1P 3BT, tel: 020 7925 6086, fax: 020 7925 6988.
Standards and Effectiveness Unit, Department for Education and Employment, Sanctuary Buildings, Great Smith Street, Westminster, London SW1P 3BT, tel: 020 7925 5000, fax: 020 7925 6000.

Target setting

Behind the jargon

When Blaise Pascal, the French philosopher, wrote 'I have made this letter longer than usual, only because I have not had the time to make it shorter', he could almost have been alluding to an important aspect of target setting in which brevity is the essence. There are two main types of targets of concern to the secondary school: output or outcome targets and input targets.

Outcome targets may be defined in terms of pupils' achievement. For example, a school may have a target such as, 'to increase the percentage of pupils getting grade C or better at General Certificate of Secondary Education (GCSE) in mathematics to x per cent by the year 2001'. Another outcome target may concern the destinations of school leavers such as the percentage seeking employment who are successful or the percentage going on to higher and further education. Yet another outcome target may relate to pupil self-esteem or other attributes and attitudes so long as a measure of them can be agreed. Such targets are typified by having clear measurable criteria and a time limit in which they will be achieved. They may be directed at:

- higher performing pupils;
- lower performing pupils, for example expressed in terms of a smaller percentage of pupils getting no GCSEs; or
- average performance, for example raising the average GCSE score per pupil, although here the spread of scores is also important.

Input targets may relate to introducing a new approach to a subject. Although input targets seem at first 'softer' than outcome targets, they should have criteria for success, which enhance their precision. So, where a new scheme of work is being introduced, the target may be expressed in terms like, 'By 2001, all teachers will be using the specified scheme for half of all French lessons'.

All schools are required to set and publish targets for raising their pupils' levels of achievement in National Curriculum tests and in public examinations and qualifications at age 16. Government, LEAs and schools work together to 'secure accountability' at each level. The LEA supports and challenges schools to ensure that targets are 'realistic and challenging'.

Each LEA reports on these targets in its Education Development Plan. The Secretary of State then satisfies himself that the schools in the LEA are aiming high enough to contribute fully towards the attainment of national targets. From July 1997 the government consulted on regulations to be made under the Education Act 1997 on target setting in schools. Schools and LEAs were consulted about the proposed value-added national system and about the 'benchmark' analyses intended to help schools make like-for-like comparisons. The general framework was envisaged as the DfEE, the Qualifications and Curriculum Authority (QCA), and OfSTED working together to provide analysis at national level with LEAs and others providing local data to supplement this. As part of the national picture each autumn, the DfEE publish a national summary of results from the year's National Curriculum assessments, the results of public examinations and further analysis (Department for Education and Employment, annually).

Circular 11/98 (Department for Education and Employment, 1998) gives advice on statutory target setting in schools. Under the Education Act 1997 section 19 and subsequent regulations, governing bodies are responsible for setting and publishing targets by the end of December each year. For secondary schools, where the end of Key Stage 4 targets relate to pupil performance in GCSEs and equivalent qualifications, targets are set for two years ahead. In the year 2000 for example, targets were set in the autumn term for pupils to reach in the Summer of 2002 and in 2002 the performance of pupils against the targets is published. Secondary schools are required to set targets for:

- pupils achieving grades A* to C in five or more subjects in GCSE examinations, equivalent vocational qualifications, or a combination of both;
- pupils achieving grades A* to G in one or more subjects in GCSE examinations, equivalent vocational qualifications, or a combination of both; and
- the average point score for the school to be achieved by pupils by the end of the following school year in GCSE and equivalent vocational qualifications.

The GCSE scores range from grade A*, which equals 8, to grade G, which equals 1, with short courses assigned half the point score of a full GCSE. Part one intermediate GNVQs are given point scores of 15 (distinction), 12 (merit) and 10 (pass). Part one foundation GNVQs are given point scores of 8 (distinction), 6 (merit) and 3 (pass). Intermediate GNVQs are allocated point scores of 30 (distinction), 24 (merit) and 28 (pass) and foundation GNVQs are allocated point scores of 16 (distinction), 12 (merit) and 6 (pass).

From September 1998, each school had to have challenging targets for improvement and had to take direct responsibility for them. Governing bodies consider all the available information and discuss 'in detail' their school's targets, together with proposals from the headteacher on the necessary improvement plans to achieve them. In the Autumn 2000, the DfEE consulted on extending the scope of target setting to include targets at Key Stage 3 and for pupils with special educational needs.

School targets should be based on:

- benchmark information on the performance of similar schools, at national and local level;
- information on the rate of progress needed to achieve national targets; and
- the most recent inspection evidence.

In setting draft targets, each school takes account of the comparative data and their own previous best performance for discussion with its LEA. Schools and LEA agree targets covering a three year period and review these annually. Where the LEA cannot agree with a school on its targets, it may evoke an early warning system.

LEAs have the power to suspend a school's right to a delegated budget when the school has been the subject of a formal warning or when an OfSTED report states that the school requires special measures or has serious weaknesses. Disagreement between the school and the LEA on the level of targets set, in isolation, would not be sufficient grounds for a budget to be withdrawn. Higher standards can only be achieved if schools take responsibility for their own improvement and take ownership of the target-setting process within their institution. The final decision therefore on the level of the school's targets rests with governing bodies as it is they who have the statutory responsibility to set the targets.

The individual school targets are included in each LEA's Education Development Plan. The accumulation of the targets total the LEA's targets, which in turn have to reflect the national targets. The DfEE and the OfSTED monitor and contribute to the process to ensure targets are high and ambitious enough (section 13). The LEA's role in advising and, as necessary, challenging schools to set their sights 'at the right level' applies especially to schools which have 'coasted along' with average performance, when their 'real potential' is higher. OfSTED inspection reports should comment on whether the school's targets are appropriate and on the progress made towards them (section 14). Within a school, the use of performance analysis enables teachers to assess progress by their pupils and to change their teaching strategies accordingly.

Comparisons of performance by different subjects, classes, year groups and other factors helps schools set targets for individual pupils that take account of each pupil's starting point. These comparisons also help the headteacher to monitor the performance of classroom teachers.

To ensure that all schools deliver high standards the two external checks are that OfSTED inspects the school at least every six years and that LEAs regularly monitor performance on the basis of objective performance information. The LEA performs various tasks including agreeing annual targets for each school (section 19).

While value added information is seen as a starting point for schools to look at targets for future attainment, it does not tell schools exactly what targets they should set because it is only an analysis of current attainment. It is made clear that 'it is pupils' real attainment which influences their future progress and life chances, not measures of their progress' (paragraph 17).

What is sometimes missed in the enthusiasm for taking an industrial and business tool and applying it to education is that in setting targets, resources may have to be moved to make the target achievable. This implies that a limited set of coherently thought through targets is better than a plethora. It also suggests that targets relate closely to priorities and should therefore be tightly linked to the school improvement plan. Targets are probably best used for aspects of the school which are unlikely to happen automatically. They can then act as a focus for aspirations, the planned channelling of resources including time and the end point of an ongoing process of monitoring progress.

The school is advised to consider:

- using discriminatingly a range of relevant information in setting targets;
- taking full responsibility for target setting, as far as possible setting their own agenda; and
- using acceptable approaches to reach targets rather than ones that distort the curriculum.

References

Department for Education and Employment (annually) *The Autumn Package*, London, DfEE.
Department for Education and Employment (1998) *Circular 11/98: Target-setting in Schools*, London, DfEE.

Further reading

Department for Education and Employment (1997) *School Self Improvement: From targets to action-guidance to support effective target-setting in schools*, London, DfEE.

Addresses

Qualifications and Curriculum Authority (QCA), 29 Bolton Street, London W1Y 7PD, tel: 020 7229 1234, fax: 020 7229 8526, e-mail: info@qca.org.uk

Standards and Effectiveness Unit, Department for Education and Employment, Sanctuary Buildings, Great Smith Street, Westminster, London SW1P 3BT, tel: 020 7925 5119, fax: 020 7925 6001, e-mail: improving.schools.dfee@gtnet. gov.uk

Thinking skills and research skills

'The most fluent talkers or the most plausible reasoners are not always the justest thinkers' considered William Hazlitt, the lucid and entertaining essayist. Bertrand Russell the philosopher was blunter: 'Many people would sooner die than think. In fact they do.'

Nickerson (1988) distinguished seven aspects of thinking.

1. processes that are involved when one thinks;
2. declarative knowledge;
3. knowledge of the normative principles of reasoning;
4. the use of higher-order tools of thought;
5. metacognitive knowledge of one's thinking processes and the ability to monitor and bring under executive control one's battery of knowledge and cognitive strategies;
6. attitudes and dispositions conducive to thinking; and
7. the effect of beliefs upon actions relating to acquiring thinking skills.

Among the processes that are involved when one thinks are organising and observing. These suggest education in what is important enough to observe and how one organises. Declarative knowledge is specific to the subject being studied for example the knowledge of oxbow lakes in geography. Knowledge of the normative principles of reasoning includes such concepts as logic. The use of higher-order tools of thought embraces such phenomena as developing strategies or training and assisting pupils to find out things for themselves (heuristics). Metacognitive knowledge of our thinking processes refers to the knowledge that we know. The ability to monitor and bring under executive control knowledge and cognitive strategies follows from this. Attitudes and dispositions conducive to thinking are influenced by the school's work in developing an ethos and high expectations that encourage all members of the school community to value learning. The effect of beliefs upon actions relating to acquiring thinking skills include, for example, self-confidence.

Views on all kinds of matters may vary. Although Elgar's A flat symphony has its admirers, Sir Thomas Beecham regarded it as 'the musical equivalent to St Pancras Station'. In the sphere of fashion, some members of Regency society considered a certain young buck to be so well dressed that he has turned people's heads. Beau Brummell commented, 'In that case, he was not well dressed.'

In the domain of thinking skills, two views are apparent. On the one hand, there is support for a skills-based or direct teaching model. On the other hand there is credence for an 'infusion' model. While the preferred approach, because of its practicability in the secondary school, is that of infusion, we need firstly to consider the skills-based approach.

Those supporting the skills-based approach argue that the requisite techniques and ways of working are teachable only if thinking is a discrete curriculum subject. One well-known approach in this mould is that of Feuerstein which recommends several years of twice weekly lessons of an 'Instrumental Enrichment' cognitive programme (Feuerstein et al., 1980).

Feuerstein's theory of learning 'structural cognitive modifiability' seeks to explain how effective cognition works, bringing in interpersonal and intrapersonal aspects of cognitive development. An important feature is the social interaction between 'experts', such as parents, teachers and peers who know more than the learner, and the 'novice'. Through 'mediation' experts structure the learning experiences of novices so that they are able to be more independent thinkers and learners. The activities and experiences that the experts present to the learners are named 'mediated learning experiences'. A cognitive map comprises the elements central to the performance of a mental act. They are as follows:

1. the content around which the mental act is centred;
2. the modality in which the mental act is expressed;
3. the degree of complexity of the task;
4. the degree of abstraction;
5. the level of efficiency with which the mental act is performed;
6. the cognitive actions required by the mental act; and
7. the learning phase.

The content around which the mental act is centred might be that of a curriculum subject such as history. The modality in which the mental act is expressed includes writing, speech, pictures, symbols and numbers. The degree of complexity of the task clearly influences the mental act and may suggest strategies for simplifying complexity. The degree of abstraction again influences the performance of the mental act and implies that practical and concrete experience may assist the learner in dealing with abstractions. The level of efficiency with which the mental act is performed may refer to the speed of the processing or the suitability of the outcome.

The cognitive actions required by the mental act will also impact upon the performance. The learning phase refers to the sequence of events through which the learner passes in carrying out the mental act.

This approach formed the basis of the construction of a form of assessment called the Learning Potential Assessment Device and the thinking skills programme, Instrumental Enrichment. In the United Kingdom, Blagg (1991) responded to the perceived limitations of Feurstein's approach in the transfer of:

- learning thinking skills through Instrumental Enrichment, to
- applying the skills across a range of curriculum subjects.

This led to the development of the Somerset Thinking Skills programme. Blagg and his colleagues distinguished between cognitive resources and cognitive strategies. Cognitive resources comprise the four domains of:

- conceptual understanding
- skills and procedures
- knowledge and experience
- verbal tools.

Cognitive strategies are higher-level general control processes. These are to do with selecting and co-ordinating specific cognitive resources for specific purposes. Eight strategic domains have been identified:

- gathering and organising
- recognising and defining
- generating alternative approaches
- planning
- monitoring and checking
- communicating
- transferring and generalising
- evaluating strategies and solutions.

Having looked at the skills-based or direct-teaching model, we can now turn to a consideration of the infusion model. In this model, effective thinking is developed through reconstructing the content and approaches to teaching aspects of curriculum subjects. The material may be presented differently and changes may be necessary to the nature of the learning tasks and the form of pupil responses. This view regards with scepticism the model that thinking can (or should) be taught distinctly separate from curriculum subjects. The infusion model seeks to incorporate knowledge about successful thinking and problem solving into teaching approaches and learning styles in each subject of the curriculum. It is dispersed or applied rather than discrete.

This model has been applied to many curriculum areas, including history, art, music, a modern foreign language, science and mathematics. It has been developed in the areas of language and literacy, reading and in the development of life skills for pupils with severe learning difficulties. These approaches tend to take a social constructivist view of the learning process. Essentially, this emphasises the importance of the learner making sense of the world in a personal way. It follows that pupils need a range of cognitive and metacognitive skills to help them comprehend the information facing them.

An important aspect of such approaches is the interaction between the teacher and the learner. The teacher is seen as a mediator between the learner and the area of learning that he or she approaches. Other learners of course can also be mediators in group work for example so long as there is sufficient structure. Mediation includes such activities as teachers helping learners to recognise the value and significance of the learning activities.

Some aspects of thinking appear to be free of the domains in which they operate and may apply to several subject domains. For example, in Nickerson's list cited earlier, 'attitudes and dispositions conducive to thinking' are important to all domains. By contrast, 'declarative knowledge specific to the subject being studied' is typical of the particular subject concerned, whether this is mathematics or art, although there are areas that overlap, for instance in mathematics, physics and art.

While there are domain-free aspects of developing thinking and these aspects are found in all subjects, it does not follow that these aspects would be better taught discretely. Indeed, if they are widely permeating, they should be taught within each subject to reinforce their importance to that subject and to wider thinking.

The school is advised to consider:

- the nature of thinking skills and develop this understanding through in-service education and training and through other means;
- planning to incorporate thinking skills into the subjects of the curriculum; and
- creating a whole school ethos in which the teachers encourage thinking and celebrate it.

References

Blagg, N. (1991) *Can We Teach Intelligence? A Comprehensive Evaluation of Feuerstein's Instrumental Enrichment Programme*, Hillsdale, N.J., Erlbaum.

Burden, R. (1998) in Burden, R. and Williams, M. (Eds.) *Thinking Through the Curriculum*, London, Routledge.

Feuerstein, R., Rand, Y., Hoffman, M. B. and Miller, R. (1980) *Instrumental Enrichment*, Baltimore, University Park Press.

Nickerson, R. S. (1988) 'On improving thinking through instruction' *Review of Research in Education* 15, 3–57.

Further reading

Hornsby, G., Atkinson, M. and Howard, J. (1997) 'Instrumental enrichment: Is this the answer to raising achievement in our schools?' *Controversial Issues in Special Education*, London, David Fulton.

Addresses

National Association for Able Children in Education (NACE), Westminster College, Harcourt Hill, Oxford OX2 9AT, tel: 01865 247 644, fax: 01865 251 847.
National Association for Gifted Children, Elder House, Milton Keynes MK9 1LR, tel: 01908 673 677, fax: 0908 673 679, e-mail: nagc@rmplc.co.uk

Transition from primary to secondary school

Securing successful transfer

There may be some truth in Samuel Butler's view of progress when he said that, 'All progress is based upon a universal innate desire on the part of every organism to live beyond its income.' But many educators would more easily subscribe to the perspective of the historian Edward Gibbon, that, 'All that is human must retrograde if it does not advance.'

At the heart of concerns about transition is that pupils make a smooth change from their primary to their secondary school and that their progress is not hampered by the change, rather that it is advanced. With this in mind, the transition from primary to secondary school can be eased by a series of steps.

Information sharing should involve a system of meetings with colleagues from secondary schools to discuss issues and particular children as necessary. Documents need to be passed on at an agreed time, with an agreed content and in an agreed way (e.g. hand to hand, e-mail). The information sharing must be monitored both to ensure that it happens and to seek ways of simplifying and improving the procedures. Parents should be involved and made aware of the contacts between primary and secondary school.

In their final year at primary school, pupils should be able to visit the secondary school that they will attend, either for a look around or/and to experience a lesson there. The secondary school will probably have its own induction system and may choose to open only for Year 7 pupils on the first day of the new school year.

From 1997, the National Curriculum tests at the end of Key Stage 2 provided fuller information on pupils' attainment in Year 6 than previously. This information is potentially useful to the teachers of the pupils as they start Year 7, although the sharing of this information between primary and secondary schools is voluntary. Year 7 teachers in secondary schools have said that they do not receive sufficiently detailed information on pupils entering Year 7 to inform their planning. However, the outcomes of the National Curriculum assessments at the end of Key Stage 2 appear to be insufficiently used to ensure the smooth progress of pupils moving from Year 6 to Year 7.

Test and teacher assessment levels in English, mathematics and science for each pupil must statutorily be passed to the receiving school. Also, additional information is available for optional use:

- test scores and the level thresholds for the tests;
- age-standardised scores;
- separate levels from the tests for reading and writing; and
- separate teacher assessment levels for each attainment target.

There is no statutory requirement for this extra information to be passed to receiving secondary schools.

Locally, schools should agree the dates in the summer term when statutory assessment data will be transferred. Schools should agree what will be included: raw test scores, age-standardised scores, separate levels for reading and writing and teacher assessment judgements relating to attainment targets.

Raw test scores allow teachers to rank order pupils. Age-standardised scores allow the attainment of pupils to be shown in relation to others of the same age with all pupils having birthdays in each month being treated as a separate sample so that the scores reflect the age of the pupil. Separate levels can be obtained for reading and writing in the end of Key Stage tests for English. Teacher assessments in the form of individual attainment levels provide information about a pupil's strengths and weaknesses in a subject and are helpful to secondary schools who can then plan work at the suitable level of difficulty in each aspect of a subject. Commercially produced standardised tests are used by many secondary schools in Year 7 to establish reading 'ages' to inform the placement of pupils in classes and subject groups and to set a baseline of attainment. Tests at the end of Key Stage 2 may now provide the information that secondary schools need.

Timing and good quality information is important to enable secondary schools to use the information to inform their decisions about the grouping of pupils. Cross-key-stage computer software allows the electronic transfer of information between primary feeder schools and secondary schools. Software also allows diagnostic use to be made of pupils' responses in each item of the end of Key Stage 2 tests through the use of an optical mark reader (OMR).

Assessment information can also inform curriculum planning and can help ensure that pupils are set work that is sufficiently demanding. Secondary schools may store the pupils' score levels at the end of Key Stage 2 and can then compare these with subsequent scores at the end of Key Stage 3. It is then possible to track the average progress that pupils make at the end of Key Stage 3 and identify and monitor pupils who make better or poorer progress. One point of doing this is to try to identify the reasons, for instance quality of teaching or pupil behaviour, which may explain the differences and take action to maintain good pupil progress and improve poor pupil progress (School Curriculum and Assessment Authority, 1997).

Nicholls and Gardner (1999) provide a useful summary of the elements of a liaison programme. These include:

- agreeing school-based objectives for the liaison programme;
- identifying a liaison teacher with the necessary qualities such as good communication skills; and
- deciding the necessary provision for acclimatising and inducting pupils, supplying information to parents, and liaising with colleagues in partner schools.

Among initiatives aimed at ensuring that transition is successful are summer literacy and numeracy schools for 11-year-olds which are linked to the Key Stage 3 programmes of participating schools. Training for head-teachers and teachers in literacy in the summer of 1999 and in numeracy in the summer of 2000 was aimed at enabling pupils to have a fast start or to catch up in their first secondary year where they may have slipped back. Key Stage 3 optional schemes of work related to the new National Curriculum were available from April 2000. Through the 'Excellence in Cities' initiative, provision for 'gifted pupils' in conurbations is meant to accelerate improvement. Learning mentors will seek to lift barriers to learning for some pupils.

The underlying concern in primary to secondary transfer is that secondary schools may not be giving sufficient emphasis to attainment at Key Stage 3. There is evidence that expectations are too low at Year 7, that there is a loss of pace in Year 8 and a relative lack of 'value added'. The highest proportion of poor teaching was in Key Stage 3 according to Her Majesty's Chief Inspector of Schools' Annual Report in 1999. Leadership and priorities set in Key Stage 3 have been seen as areas for improvement. Years 7 to 9 should be seen as essential steps to achievement. Pupils should learn to think creatively and rigorously and should feel part of the school community, for example by ensuring that academic and pastoral structures work together. Targets can be set for each pupil in Key Stage 3 (Barber, 1999).

The North of England Conference speech by the Secretary of State for Education and Employment (Department for Education and Employment, 2000) set out the new challenges as seen by the government. These are easing the transition of children from one stage of education to another, and improving performance at key stage 3. Policies were intended to address the issue of high expectations and ensure that the new founda-tions in literacy, numeracy and science are built on from the entry into secondary education. Approaches include new optional English and mathematics tests for all 12-year-olds. Schools would set targets for achievements in these tests in December 2000 for the year 2002. Transfer data between primary and secondary schools would be improved and secondary teachers would undergo retraining to strengthen teaching, improve subject knowledge and make teaching 'more inspiring'. A numeracy and a literacy framework for Year 7 similar to those at primary level was to be published to assist secondary teachers.

The school is advised to consider:

- focusing on strategies that aid the transfer process and allow it to plan appropriate work for Key Stage 3; and
- ensuring that, although statutory targets relate to Key Stage 4, due importance is placed on Key Stage 3 both in itself and as a stepping stone to high attainment later.

References

Barber, M. (1999) 'Outcome depends on the middle years' *Times Educational Supplement* 1 October, p. 17.

Department for Education and Employment (2000) *Raising Aspirations in the 21st Century*, London, DfEE.

Nicholls, G. and Gardner, J. (1999) *Pupils in Transition: Moving between key stages*, London, Routledge.

School Curriculum and Assessment Authority (1997) *Making Effective Use of Key Stage 2 Assessments at the Transfer Between Key Stage 2 and Key Stage 3 to Support Teaching of Pupils in Year 7: A guide to good practice*, London, SCAA.

Further reading

School Curriculum and Assessment Authority (1996) *Promoting Continuity Between Key Stage 2 and Key Stage 3*, London, SCAA.

Addresses

Qualifications and Curriculum Authority (QCA), 29 Bolton Street, London W1Y 7PD, tel: 020 7229 1234, fax: 020 7229 8526, e-mail: info@qca.org.uk

Key Solutions RM Ltd., Wharfe House, Ilkley Road, Otley, West Yorkshire LS21 3JP, tel: 01943 463 346.

SIMS Education Services Ltd., The SIMS Centre, Stannard Way, Priory Business Park, Cardington, Bedford, MK44 3SG, tel: 01234 838 990.

Value added
Support or illumination?

It is easy to be dismissive of statistical information. Andrew Lang spoke of someone, 'using statistics as a drunken man uses lamp-posts, for support rather than illumination'. A more generous and perhaps a more balanced view is given by the British medical doctor Noel Moynihan who said, 'Statistics can prove anything, even the truth.' So it is with value-added measures. They may be able to approach the truth if care is taken in their use and interpretation and in particular in their dissemination.

Schools that come out top in academic performance league tables take value-added measures in their stride. Such schools may see league tables as a way of indicating how they have succeeded in relation to the assessment used: usually examination results. Schools that perform in absolute terms less well than others in academic performance are worried about league tables. They are keen to explain why they might be being unfairly relegated to the lower reaches of the tables. This concern over league tables and the worry that they oversimplify the relative success or failure of a school has led to an interest in one aspect of value-added analysis.

The limitations of comparing schools according to raw results without sufficiently taking into account other factors has long been recognised (e.g. Mortimore *et al.*, 1988). It is widely accepted that the attainment of a pupil is in part owing to the effectiveness of the school but is also influenced by social circumstances and the educational experiences of his or her parents.

Also, the assessments of attainment used to indicate the progress that can be more confidently be attributed to the school should be broad. They should include not only test results but also cultural and sporting achievements, community achievements and the destinations of school leavers, including careers and further and higher education.

Currently, league tables and some value-added analyses concentrate on examination and test results and on attendance. Less attention has been paid to pupil attitudes relating to pupil attainment. Similarly, less work has been carried out on aspects of performance that are important in employment as well as in school, such as problem solving, flexibility, creativity and co-operation.

This approach seeks to enable so-called fair comparisons of schools to be made. It gives estimates of the average progress of each school. One has to adjust for certain factors and for prior attainment by the individual child. It is important to get the appropriate measures to use in analysing educational outcomes and these range from the aggregation of academic results and attendance figures to multilevel modelling techniques. An important aspect of the technique is that it looks at the value that would be anticipated if only expected progress were made. The most important indicator of pupil achievement is pupil prior attainment and this has led to the introduction of baseline assessment and on-entry assessment.

Pupils in Year 7 may be tested using Cognitive Abilities Tests (CATS) by the National Foundation of Educational Research and the Middle Years Information Service (MIDYIS). Year 9 pupils are assessed through the National Curriculum Tests and Tasks. In Years 10 and 11 the Year Eleven Information Service (YELLIS) from Durham University is used. In the sixth form, the A Level Information Service (ALIS) from Durham University is used. All these, of course, predict within certain levels of confidence the outcome for pupils and cohorts in public examinations.

The National Foundation for Educational Research undertakes analysis of examinations through its Education Resources Education Centre (ERIC) and through using the Quantitative Analysis of Self Evaluation (QUASE). Information from the Office for Standards in Education (OfSTED) is also important in relation to value-added analyses, for example the 'Performance AND Assessment' report (PANDA).

Value-added analyses do not solve the problems of league tables by creating adjusted league tables and results still need to be interpreted with care. The effects that a school has cannot easily be separated statistically from the differences between schools that would be expected by chance. Only where there are great differences between schools can the effect of what a particular school is doing be considered with sufficient confidence as influential to contributing to that difference.

Also, the power of the newspaper headline or the top story of the radio or television news cannot be overestimated. Any headteacher facing a headline that places his school at the bottom of a league table has a difficult task. He or she has to persuade parents and others to read the fine print of a value-added analysis which indicates that if all background factors and pupil prior attainment is taken into account, the school made better progress than the school at the top of the table. People tend not to listen to the success stories of runners who come second.

Ambitious parents are often more interested in overall academic achievement and the opportunities that are offered by a school where students leave with high academic qualifications rather than a school that offers 'better' progress for the lower-performing student. Employers and parents also know the power of qualifications in the employment market-place and will require a good deal of convincing that value-added in attitudes, co-operation and creativity can count for as much as a sheaf of Advanced levels or well-respected vocational qualifications.

However, value-added measures are not only applied to whole school measures, but have a role as a management tool to compare individual teachers, departments and aspects of school life. These can be used to explore any differences in, say, the relative progress of mathematics groups, pupils with special educational needs, girls compared with boys and a variety of other indicators. What is important is the way in which results are used and the quality of the professional dialogue and action which they generate. In this respect, value-added data contributes to measures of school effectiveness and can potentially lead to school improvement. They may increase the accountability of teachers and others and, if professionally followed through, may raise standards.

A particular issue arises with regard to pupils identified as having special educational needs (SENs). It appears at first as though the number of pupils with SENs should be taken into account when considering value added. Given that such children have learning difficulties, it seems only fair that this is recognised when judging the progress that a school has made from a specified baseline. This is not however as straightforward as it at first seems. Under the system that exists in the *Code of Practice on the Identification and Assessment of Special Educational Needs* (Department for Education, 1994) schools identify pupils as having SENs. This means in practice that there is considerable variation in the level of learning difficulty considered to require special educational provision from school to school. A school with say 20 per cent of children on its register of pupils with SENs may not be comparable with another school which also has 20 per cent of pupils on the SEN register. One possible way to address this difficulty is to consider whether the majority of pupils with SENs could be considered in terms of the standards they have reached and the progress they have made in specified period. This would enable schools to see if pupils on their SEN register were comparable in terms of standards and, if they were, then (all other things being equal) comparisons of subsequent progress for these pupils could be made with similar schools.

The school is advised to consider:

- Using and disseminating value-added information that gives as clear an indication as possible of the school's effect on pupil attainment;
- The rationale behind any approaches to value added and the assumptions made by the model used; and
- The importance of 'raw attainment' scores as an indication of the level at which the pupils are working.

References

Department for Education (1994) *Code of Practice on the Identification and Assessment of Special Educational Needs*, London, DFE.

Mortimore, P., Sammons, P., Stoll, L., Lewis, D. and Ecob, R. (1988) *School Matters*, Wells: Open Books.

Further reading

McPherson, A. (1992) *Measuring Value Added in Schools* National Commission on Education Briefing No.1, London, National Commission on Education Briefing.

Addresses

Qualifications and Curriculum Authority (QCA), 29 Bolton Street, London W1Y 7PD, tel: 020 7229 1234, fax: 020 7229 8526, e-mail: info@qca.org.uk

National Foundation for Educational Research (NFER), The Mere, Upton Park, Slough, Windsor, Berkshire SL1 2DQ, tel: 01753 574 123, fax: 01753 691 632, web-site: www.nfer.ac.uk

Very able pupils

Improving their attainment and contribution to the school

Lord Macauley, the historian, taking perhaps a sentimental view of intellect, stated, 'The highest intellects, like the tops of mountains, are the first to catch and reflect the dawn.' At the other extreme, the British writer Gerald Brenan considered intellectuals to be 'people who believe that ideas are of more importance than values. That is to say, their own ideas and other peoples values.' In any event, when one considers the very able, one is not only considering intellect but a range of possible areas of human achievement in which the person excels. This may include, for example, leadership and social and personal abilities as well as intellectual abilities.

From the point of view of terminology, the term, 'gifted' can be unhelpful because it may be taken to imply that the gift was discrete and self-contained and was given by someone, perhaps an omniscient being. The term may also unfairly convey the impression that the very able person is merely exercising a given gift that has required little dedication and hard work to demonstrate, an impression very far from the usual reality. Also, the word 'genius' has unhelpful connotations and, in any case, is usually reserved for adults who have contributed significantly to the world. A helpful definition is provided by Freeman (1998), who regards the very able as those 'who demonstrate exceptionally high levels of performance, whether across a limited field, or those whose potential for excellence has not been recognised either by tests or experts'.

If as a guide, the term 'very able' is applied to about 5 per cent of pupils in a secondary school, then all other things being equal, a typical class of thirty pupils would contain one or two very able pupils. Related to defining the term 'very able' is the issue of identification. Among the ways of identifying very able children are intelligence tests, recommendation by teachers, or parents and peer nomination. Very able pupils may have certain characteristics that help identify their ability. Among these are acute powers of observation, fluency with words and an extensive vocabulary, originality, imagination and creativity, quickness and agility in thought, responsiveness to fresh ideas, a good memory, a quick grasp of abstract concepts and the ability to apply such concepts easily. Other pointers include superior reasoning ability, the ability to generalise from specific instances, the ability to recognise connections and patterns and to extrapolate from them, and high-level cognitive skills, including evaluation, synthesis, analysis and logic. Other indicators that a pupil may be very able are: intellectual curiosity, having many interests, having extensive interest and knowledge in one, some, or all subjects, the ability to concentrate for long periods and the capacity to give sustained interest to a subject.

An innovative way of identifying very able pupils is through provision. An example of this approach is found in the Szold Institute in Jerusalem. Here consideration is given to the outcomes of exposing children to opportunities in the visual arts and in sciences. The assessment process involves teacher ratings of pupil behaviour, task performance and the professional evaluation of pupil portfolios (Zorman, 1997). Particular care needs to be taken in the case of very able pupils who may be hiding or disguising their ability through inappropriate or evasive behaviour for whatever reason.

Identification is not always straightforward, however. Very able pupils may behave in the classroom in a way that does not lead the teacher to think immediately in terms of high ability. For example, to the hard-pressed teacher, a pupil who asks unusual questions, who has more knowledge in certain areas than the teacher herself, or who presses issues with great persistence may appear threatening rather than enriching. Also the abilities of very able pupils may be concealed. The reasons for this include pupils hiding their abilities so as not to stand out too much from the crowd or pupils lacking the necessary stimulation. Other factors may be the inability of the pupil to write as quickly as he can think leading to dissatisfaction with writing and consequently avoidance of writing or feelings of frustration. Among the factors that may camouflage abilities are scepticism, impatience with oneself and an intolerance of others, lack of interest in the approval of others, inability to work co-operatively with peers, overreaction to disapproval, lack of co-operation, and so on.

Once very able pupils are identified, the appropriate provision is important. Among the important features of provision are varied teaching and learning styles, flexibility and adaptability in the pace of learning and breadth and balance of the curriculum.

Teachers must make clear to very able pupils the requirements relating to tasks that are intended to challenge them. For example, if an extension task is given to a pupil, the teacher should be clear that this is intended to extend the challenge to the pupil not to extend the time. It should be made clear to the pupil that he is expected to complete the work done by the rest of the class and also to complete the extension task in the same time that others are working on the main task, if this is what the teacher intends. Otherwise the pupil may pace himself to complete the main class work and not reach the extension task.

Enrichment enables a pupil to deepen and extend knowledge of a given area through supplementary tasks but may require the teacher to make a creative contribution for the task to be particularly beneficial. Subject leaders may be best placed to advise colleagues on the nature and content of enriching tasks.

When the question of grouping pupils arises, a balance is often sought. On the one hand there are the needs of the very able pupil to be with others operating at similar levels, for example for an outstanding athlete to practice with others who are also performing at a high level. On the other hand, there is a need for the very able pupil to be with peers whom he knows and who support him socially. Grouping should be sufficiently flexible to allow for intellectual stimulation as well as for the social development of interactive communication skills.

Good teacher questioning of pupils through sufficiently challenging, open-ended questions is important. In whole class teaching closed questions maintain a brisk pace but may not be sufficiently challenging for very able pupils. Open-ended questions may slow the pace but may stretch the very able more. Again a balance needs to be struck. Another way of maintaining pace yet providing challenge is to provide the very challenging questions to very able pupils in group work either through small-group questions from the teacher or through differentiated written questions.

A whole school written policy is one way of summarising the aspirations of the school for its very able pupils and of setting out the practical things that will happen to meet their educational requirements. A policy could helpfully include (Ayer, 1995):

- a general rationale;
- the aims of the policy which should be revisited to ensure that they are achieved;
- definitions including a clear definition of the very able pupil;
- the general overall approach of the school;
- identification and monitoring schemes;
- organisational responses (such as acceleration);
- the in-class approach (for example enrichment and extension);
- out-of-class activities;
- personal and social organisation;
- responsibility for co-ordinating and monitoring;
- the process for review and monitoring; and
- the use of outside agencies (for example for provision and training).

National Association for Gifted Children (1998) set out the elements of a whole school policy which include:

- the aims of the school related to the very able policy;
- staff responsibilities;
- the definition of pupils to be included;
- identification strategies (evidence from home; evidence from former schools; discussion with the pupil; results of tests; assessment, record keeping and the transfer of records; awareness of the features of high ability); and
- curriculum policies (setting; differentiation including enrichment, extension and withdrawal; acceleration; library and resources policy; teaching and learning styles; homework policy; marking and assessment policy).

In June 1998, the Schools Standards Minister, Estelle Morris, announced an expansion of the number and scope of the specialist school programme involving an additional fifty-one schools to join the programme, while specialist schools would offer pilot master classes to develop the talents of 'gifted and talented children'. In September of the same year Estelle Morris launched a new advisory group on 'gifted and talented' children. The group advises government on how best to identify and support the needs of 'gifted' children, devising a strategy to release these children's potential. The group set out to explore how schools can maintain an ethos that celebrates excellence and rewards high achievement. The White Paper *Excellence in Schools* had announced the government's intention to develop a strategy for the early identification and support of particularly able and talented children.

In March 1999 the government announced an action plan for inner-city education, 'Excellence in Cities', aiming to raise standards and aspirations in the bigger cities. This included an approach to meet the needs of 'gifted and talented' children and to develop 'world class tests' to stretch the 'most able' children and young people.

The school is advised to consider:

- developing and regularly revising a policy for very able pupils which reflects national and local initiatives and relevant research; and
- reviewing all procedures and approaches in the school to ensure that, as appropriate, they enhance the learning of very able pupils.

References

Ayre, D. (1995) *School Governors and More Able Children*, London, Department for Education and Employment.

Freeman, J. (1998) *Educating the Very Able: Current international research*, London, Office for Standards in Education.

National Association for Gifted Children (1998) *Help With Bright Children*, Milton Keynes, NAGC.

Zorman, R. (1997) 'Eureka: the cross cultural model for identification of hidden talent through enrichment' *Roeper Review* 20, 54–61.

Further reading

Eyre, D. (1997) *Able Children in Ordinary Schools*, London, David Fulton.

Addresses

National Association for Able Children in Education (NACE), Westminster College, Harcourt Hill, Oxford OX2 9AT, tel: 01865 247 644, fax: 01865 251 847.
National Association for Gifted Children (NAGC), Elder House, Milton Keynes MK9 1LR, tel: 01908 673 677, fax: 01908 673 679, e-mail: nagc@rmplc.co.uk

Glossary (selective)

Beacon school A school of recognised excellence funded to work with other schools to share good practice.

CAD/CAM CAD is computer-aided design. CAM is computer-aided manufacture. CAD/CAM is an important aspect of the Key Stage 4 programme of study for design and technology.

City Academies City Academies take over from or replace seriously failing schools and are built and managed by partnerships of the government and voluntary, church and business sponsors. They may offer new approaches to management, governance, teaching and the curriculum, including a specialist focus in at least one curriculum area.

City Learning Centre Part of the Excellence in Cities initiative. These Centres provide study support through activities for young people and the community in the evenings, weekends and school holidays (including for the gifted and talented).

Education Action Zone (EAZ) A zone in which support is given to disadvantaged schools and communities.

Ethnic Minority and Traveller Achievement Grant A government grant to help meet the educational needs of:

- children from minority ethnic groups who may be at risk of underachieving in school;
- pupils for whom English is an additional language; and
- the children of Travellers.

Education authorities submit plans which include targets for improving the educational achievement of these groups.

Excellence in Cities Areas Areas in which partnership schools decide how resources are allocated. Schools work in clusters (e.g. on programmes for gifted and talented pupils) to share resources and good practice.

***Excellence in Schools* White Paper** The policy in the White Paper *Excellence in Schools* was to apply pressure for improvement and support for those involved in raising standards. Six principles were involved: education was at the heart of government; policies would benefit the many; the focus would be on school standards; government would intervene in underperforming schools; there would be 'zero tolerance' of underperformance; and government would work in partnership with those committed to raising standards.

Fresh Start Policy The closure of a school and its replacement with a new school. This was further developed as follows: by allowing new schools to be established within the publicly provided sector; by allowing existing private schools to be part of the publicly provided sector; and by allowing new promoters from the voluntary, business, or religious sectors to take over weak schools or replace them with City Academies.

Learning Support Units These units seek to ensure that disruptive pupils are dealt with outside the classroom.

Low Achieving Schools All schools achieving less than A* to C in General Certificate of Secondary Education examinations were from the year 2000 onwards linked with a partner school with a proven successful track record.

National Grid for Learning A means of extending the use of new technology

National Mentoring Network For pupils in lower performing schools, a pilot project from October 1999 aimed at raising the achievement of 12–16 year olds in secondary schools in deprived areas. University students as learner mentors support identified pupils in 'Education Action Zones' who are at risk. Ethnic Minority Mentoring Projects were supported by bursaries and they work in partnership with the NMN.

New Opportunities Fund Funding from the national lottery.

Schools Plus Policy Action Team This team develops proposals to further study the development of study support and school/community links in disadvantaged areas.

Specialist Schools The term 'specialist school' has two meanings. The first relates to special schools that are seeking to increase inclusion in mainstream schools by acting in part as a resources centre and in other ways. The second meaning is schools which develop expertise in the arts, languages, sports and technology (e.g. Technology Colleges) aiming to help improve standards in secondary schools as a whole. A third of funding goes towards a plan to help other schools and the community.

Standards Site A Department for Education web-site intended to share and disseminate good practice. It is based on good practice identified from successful local education authorities, for example, creating a high achievement culture in schools, supporting headteachers and governors, collecting and analysing performance data, and using advisers to give early identification of schools at risk.

Super heads   An experienced and successful headteacher works with three to five schools to help them raise standards.

Supplementary schools   A community based initiative giving support to children outside school hours. A Supplementary Schools Support Service aims to give practical support to these schools to raise educational achievement (of pupils from ethnic minority groups who may be at risk of underachieving). Related to this approach are organisations such as Education Extra (and the Community Education Development Centre).

'Teaching' Green Paper   The Green Paper *Teachers Meeting the Challenge of Change*, published by the Department for Education and Employment in 1998, concerns the development of teachers and seeks to encourage effective performance management.

Bibliography

Audit Commission (1998) *Changing Partners*, London, Stationery Office.

——(1999) *Missing Out*, London, Audit Commission.

Ayre, D. (1995) *School Governors and More Able Children*, London, DfEE.

Barber, M. (1999) 'Outcome depends on the middle years', *Times Educational Supplement*, 1 October, p. 17.

Bardsley, K., Costa, P. and Walton, J. (1999) 'The essential elements of an effective attendance policy' in E. Blyth and J. Milner (1999) *Improving School Attendance*, London, Routledge.

Berkeley, R. (1999) *Not Fitting In: Exclusions from school, a local study*, Oxford, Department of Educational Studies, University of Oxford.

Blagg, N. (1991) *Can We Teach Intelligence? A Comprehensive Evaluation of Feuerstein's Instrumental Enrichment Programme*, Hillsdale, N.J.: Erlbaum.

Bleach, K. (2000) *The Induction and Mentoring of Newly Qualified Teachers*, London, David Fulton.

Bloomer, M. (1997) *Curriculum Making in Post-16 Education: The social conditions of studentship*, London, Routledge.

Blythe, E. and Milner, J. (1999) *Improving School Attendance*, London, Routledge.

British Educational Suppliers Association (annually) *The Complete Guide to British Educational Supply*, London, BESA.

Brophy, J. E. (1979) 'Teacher behaviour and its effects' *Journal of Educational Psychology* 71, 6.

—— (1983) 'Classroom organisation and management' *The Elementary School Journal* 83, 4.

Brown, S. (1990) in T. Horton (ed.) *Assessment Debates*, Milton Keynes, The Open University Press, pp. 5–11.

Bruner, J. (1986) *Actual Minds, Possible Worlds*, Cambridge, Mass., Harvard University Press.

Burden, R. (1998) in R. Burden and M. Williams (eds) *Thinking Through the Curriculum*, London, Routledge.

Clarke, A. and Millard, E. (1998) *Gender in the Secondary Curriculum: Balancing the books*, London, Routledge.

Davies, J. (1998) 'Taking risks or playing safe' in A. Clarke and E. Millard (1998) *Gender in the Secondary Curriculum: Balancing the books*, London, Routledge.

Department for Education (1993) *Circular 9/93: Protection of Children: Disclosure of criminal background of those with access to children*, London, DFE.

—— (1994) *Code of Practice on the Identification and Assessment of Special Educational Needs*, London, DFE.

—— (1994) *Circular 1/94: Religious Education and Collective Worship*, London, DFE.

—— (1995) *Circular 10/95: Protecting Children from Abuse: The role of the education service*, London, DfEE.

Department for Education and Employment (1997) *Circular 13/97: The Standards Fund 1998–99*, London, DfEE.

—— (1997) *Circular 10/97 Teaching: High Status, High Standards: Requirements for courses of initial teacher training*, London, DfEE.

—— (1997) *Excellence in Schools (White Paper) Cm. 3681*, London, The Stationery Office.

—— (1997) *Excellence for All Children: Meeting special educational needs*, London, DfEE.

—— (1997) *School Self Improvement: From targets to action-guidance to support effective target-setting in schools*, London, DfEE.

—— (1998) *Circular 11/98: Target-Setting in Schools*, London, DfEE.

—— (1998) *Meeting Special Educational Needs: A programme of action*, London, DfEE.

—— (1998) *Circular 4/98: Teaching: High status, High standards: Requirements for courses of initial teacher training*, London, DfEE.

—— (1998) *Excellence for All Schools*, London, DfEE.

—— (1998) *Teachers Meeting the Challenge of Change*, London, DfEE.

—— (1998) *Excellence in Research on Schools, Report No. 74* [The Hillage Report], London, DfEE.

—— (1999) *Circular 10/99: Social Exclusion: Pupil support*, London, DfEE.

—— (1999) *Reviewing Performance and Pay of Heads and Deputy Heads: Guidance for governors*, London, DfEE.

—— (1999) *Performance Management Framework for Teachers: Consultation Document*, London, DfEE.

—— (1999) *Code of Practice on LEA–School Relations*, London, DfEE.

—— (1999) *The Education (Individual Pupil Information) (Prescribed Persons) Regulations 1999 (Statutory Instrument 1999 No. 903)*, London, DfEE.

—— (1999) *Circular 06/99: Schools Causing Concern*, London, DfEE.

—— (1999) *Excellence in Cities*, London, DfEE.

—— (1999) *Social Inclusion: Pupil support*, London, DfEE.

—— (1999) *Tackling Truancy*, London, DfEE.

—— (1999) *Consultation Document on Governors' Regulations*, London, DfEE.

—— (2000) *Raising Aspirations in the 21st Century*, London, DfEE.

—— (annually) *The Autumn Package*, London, DfEE.

Department for Education, Home Office, Department for Health (1991) *Working Together Under the Children Act 1989: A guide to arrangements for interagency co-operation for the protection of children from abuse*, London, Department for Education, Home Office, Department for Health.

Department for Education and Employment and Office for Standards in Education (1997) *From Targets to Action: Guidance to support effective target setting in schools (Improving Schools Series)*, London, DfEE, Standards and Effectiveness Unit.

—— (1999) *DfEE/OfSTED Guidance Notes on Preparing an Action Plan and a LEA Commentary and Statement of Action for a School Under Special Measures*, London, DfEE/ OfSTED.

Department for Education and Employment/Department for Trade and Industry/ Standards and Effectiveness Unit (1999) *Connect for Better Schools: Schools securing the future* (CD-ROM; A4 file; library disk), London, DfEE/DTI/SEU.

Education Year Book (annually), London, Pitman.

Eyre, D. (1997) *Able Children in Ordinary Schools*, London, David Fulton.

Farrell, M., Kerry, T. and Kerry, C. (1995) *The Blackwell Handbook of Education*, Oxford, Blackwell.

Farrell, M. (1998) *The Special Education Handbook*, London, David Fulton.

Feuerstein, R., Rand, Y., Hoffman, M. B. and Miller, R. (1980) *Instrumental Enrichment*, Baltimore, Md., University Park Press.

Freeman, J. (1998) *Educating the Very Able: Current international research*, London, OfSTED.

Further Education Development Agency (1999) *Recruiting Tomorrow's Workforce: How employers can support GNVQs in schools and colleges*, London, FEDA.

Gann, N. (1998) *Improving School Governance: How better governors make better schools*, London, Falmer Press.

Harlen, W. (1991) 'National curriculum assessment: increasing the benefit by reducing the burden' in *Education and Change in the 1990s*, Journal of the Educational Research Network of Northern Ireland No. 5, February, 3–19.

Harlen, W., Gipps, C., Broadfoot, P. and Nuttall, D. (1992) 'Assessment and the improvement of education' *The Curriculum Journal* 3, 3, 215–230.

Her Majesty's Inspectors (1999) *Raising the Attainment of Ethnic Minority Pupils: School and LEA Responses, HMI 170*, London.

Hornsby, G., Atkinson, M. and Howard, J. (1997) 'Instrumental enrichment: Is this the answer to raising achievement in our schools?' in *Controversial Issues in Special Education*, London, David Fulton.

Institute of Development Professional in Education (1999) *Principles and Standards of Professional Practice*, Manchester, IDP.

Johnson, B. (1999) 'Raising Expectations at Don Valley High School' in E. Blyth and J. Milner (1999) *Improving School Attendance*, London, Routledge.

Kerry, T. and Price, G. (1996) 'The classroom: Organisation, effectiveness and Resources' in M. Farrell (ed.) *Distance Education for Teaching*, Reading, Centre for British Teachers.

Kilfoyle. P. (1997) *Every Child Is Special: Proposals to improve special needs education*, London, Labour Party.

McPherson, A. (1992) *Measuring Value Added in Schools*, National Commission on Education Briefing No.1, London, National Commission on Education Briefing.

Mortimore, P., Sammons, P., Stoll, L., Lewis, D. and Ecob, R. (1988) *School Matters*, Wells, Open Books.

National Association of Careers and Guidance Teachers (1998) *Raising Achievement: The contribution of careers education and guidance*, Monmouth, NACGT.

National Association for Gifted Children (1998) *Help With Bright Children*, Milton Keynes, NAGC.

National Consumer Council (1996) *Sponsorship in Schools: Good Practice Guidelines*, London, NCC.

National Institute for Careers Education and Counselling (1997) *Managing Careers Work in Schools*, Cambridge, NICEC.

National Society for the Prevention of Cruelty to Children (1989) *Protecting Children: A guide for teachers on child abuse*, London, NSPCC.

Nicholls, G. and Gardner, J. (1999) *Pupils in Transition: Moving between key stages*, London, Routledge.

Nickerson, R. S. (1988) 'On improving thinking through instruction' *Review of Research in Education* 15, 3–57.

Office for Standards in Education (1994) *Improving Schools*, London, Her Majesty's Stationery Office.

—— (1998) *School Evaluation Matters*, London, OfSTED.

—— (1998) *National Survey of Careers Education and Guidance*, London, OfSTED.

—— (1999) *Lessons Learned from Special Measures*, London, OfSTED.

—— (1999) *LEA Support for School Improvement*, London, OfSTED.

—— (1999) *Handbook for Inspecting Secondary Schools with Guidance on Self-Evaluation*, London: The Stationery Office.

Priestly, J. (1999) *The Essence of Education*, London, Methodist Working Party.

Qualifications and Curriculum Authority (annually) *Assessment and Reporting Arrangements*, London, QCA.

—— (1997) *Baseline Assessment Scales for Children with Special Educational Needs: Teachers Guide*, London, QCA.

—— (1998) *Education for Citizenship and the Teaching of Democracy in Schools: Final Report of the Advisory Group on Citizenship and the Teaching of Democracy in Schools* [The Crick Report], London, QCA.

—— (1999) *Learning from Work Experience*, London, QCA.

—— (1999) *Learning Outcomes from Careers Education and Guidance*, London, QCA.

Rae, J. (1998) *Letters to Parents*, London, HarperCollins.

Sallis, J. (1999) *Managing Better with Governors*, London, Financial Times Management.

Saunders, L. and Stradling, R. with Gallagher, S. (1996) *Raising Attainment in Secondary Schools: A handbook for school self evaluation*, Slough, National Foundation for Educational Research.

School Curriculum and Assessment Authority (1996) *Teaching English as an Additional language: A framework for policy*, London, SCAA.

—— (1996) *Promoting Continuity Between Key Stage 2 and Key Stage 3*, London, SCAA.

—— (1997) *Making Effective Use of Key Stage 2 Assessments at the Transfer Between Key Stage 2 and Key Stage 3 to Support Teaching of Pupils in Year 7: A guide to good practice*, London, SCAA.

—— (1997) *Baseline Assessment Scales*, London, SCAA.

Skelton, A. (1998) 'Eclipsed by Eton Fields' in A. Clarke and E. Millard (1998) *Gender in the Secondary Curriculum: Balancing the books*, London, Routledge.

Social Exclusion Unit (1998) *Truancy and School Exclusion* (Report by the Social Exclusion Unit), London, Cabinet Office.

Statutory Instrument 1999, number 2163.

Teacher Training Agency (1997) *Effective Training Through Partnership: Working papers on secondary partnership*, London, TTA.

—— (1998) *National Standards for Qualified Teacher Status, Subject Leaders, Special Educational Needs Co-ordinators and Head Teachers*, London, TTA.

—— (1998) *Initial Teacher Training Curriculum: The use of information and communications technology in subject teaching*, London, TTA.

—— (1998) *National Standards for Subject Leaders*, London, TTA.

—— (1998) *The National Standards for Headteachers*, London, TTA.

Times Educational Supplement (1999) 'Ministers told cash pays off in results', Friday 11 June 1999, No. 4328, p. 1.

University of Warwick (1999) *Directory of Teaching Materials* from Business University of Warwick Centre for Education and Industry.

Vulliamy, G. and Web, R. (1999) *Meeting Need and Challenging Crime in Partnership with Schools*, London, Home Office.

Vygotsky, L. S. (1962) *Thought and Language*, Cambridge, Mass., Massachusetts, Institute of Technology Press.

—— (1978) *Mind and Society: The development of higher psychological processes*, Cambridge, Mass., Harvard University Press.

Whitney, B. (1998) *The Complete Guide to Attendance and Absence*, London, Croner Publications.

Zorman, R. (1997) 'Eureka: the cross cultural model for identification of hidden talent through enrichment' *Roeper Review* 20, 54–61.

Examination Results

Processing, Analysis and Presentation

Michael Matthewman

At the beginning of each academic year schools are required to present their examination results to an audience of teaching staff, governors and parents. This A4 book and disk provides clear guidance for examinations officers on how to process, analyse and record these results.

The pack is specifically designed to enable the examinations officer to process the results on a PC off-site, and encourages a cumulative approach to examination results in addition to the annual statutory requirements.

The booklet includes:

- step-by-step instructions and examples
- a disk of templates which can be personalised to meet the needs of your institution
- detailed advice on compiling a Cumulative Performance Table and an annual in-school Handbook of Results.

This book and disk not only enables the examinations officer to examine and present the annual GCSE and A Level results in a coherent and cogent manner, it also provides the means for a fully comprehensive appraisal of your school's performance over a set period of time.

August 2000: 296×210: 120pp
Pb: 0–415–23226–0: £29.99

Stress Management Programme for Secondary School Students

Sarah McNamara

This is a resource pack for teachers to use in classrooms to help students combat stress. As well as the theory, it has photocopiable worksheets included. The pack covers the following areas:

- preparing for exams
- learning study skills
- building self-confidence and self-esteem
- coping with relationships and family problems
- diet and exercise issues.

The information is presented in an accessible way and there are plenty of follow-up activities and strategies for coping. Everything is geared towards making it readable and interesting for young people but it never loses sight of the needs of the curriculum.

January 2001: 296×210: 112pp
Pb: 0–415–23839–0: £29.99

Transforming Northicote School

Sir Geoff Hampton and Dr. Jeff Jones

In February 1994 Northicote School, situated in a deprived area of Wolverhampton, was the first in the country to be 'named and shamed', OFSTED called the school *'appalling in almost every way'*.

Then Geoff Hampton took over as head. Five years later he was awarded a knighthood for transforming the fortunes of this failing school and its pupils.

This manageable book pulls out the key points from the five year programme and shares successful strategies with other heads, governors and teachers.

October 2000: 216×138: 176pp
Pb: 0–415–22092–0: £12.99

Using Data for Monitoring and Target Setting

A Practical Guide for Teachers

Ray Sumner and Ian McCallum

Are you keeping track of standards in your school?

Using Data for Monitoring and Target Setting is a clear and practical guide for teachers and school administrative staff that shows how to use spreadsheets to create orderly records of assessment. These can then be used for the sort of statistical analyses which are now being demanded from schools.

This guide is photocopiable and includes:

- lots of practical examples
- step-by-step instructions on how to obtain the data you want
- simple advice on how to use EXCEL
- pictures of the actual screens you will be using.

1999: 297x210: 100pp
Pb: 0–415–19686–8: £25.00